A   P I C T O R I A L   G U I D E   T O

BILTMORE™

THE   BILTMORE   COMPANY

ASHEVILLE,   NORTH   CAROLINA

PUBLISHED BY THE BILTMORE COMPANY

One North Pack Square, Asheville, North Carolina 28801

800-543-2961 *biltmore.com*

PRODUCTION INFORMATION

Rosemary G. Rennicke, Buckingham, Pennsylvania, and Diane Maddex, Archetype Press, Inc., Washington, D.C.

Design, Prepress, and Print Coordination by Terrell Creative, Kansas City, MO.

Original Text written by Rachel D. Carley and Rosemary G. Rennicke.

Additional text by Bill Alexander, Darren Poupore, and Ellen Rickman.

Creative Direction and Editorial Support by Russell Shuler, Judy Ross, and Christy Cowan, Biltmore.

Color photographs by Bill Alexander, Tim Barnwell, Richard Brown and Assoc., Cheryl Dalton, Terry Davis, Carroll Morgan, Mike Smith, Sandra Stambaugh, James Valentine, and John Warner.

Black and white photographs from Biltmore Estate archives.

Photo on page 119 courtesy of the Frances Loeb Library, Harvard Graduate School of Design.

LIBRARY OF CONGRESS CATALOGING-IN-PUBLICATION DATA

Carley, Rachel.

A guide to Biltmore Estate / [written by Rachel Carley and Rosemary G. Rennicke].

    p.   cm.

isbn 1-885378-00-9 (hardbound) — isbn 1-885378-01-7 (paperbound)

1. Biltmore Estate (Asheville, N.C.) — Guidebooks.   2. Asheville (N.C.) — Buildings, structures, etc. — Guidebooks.   I. Title.

f264.a8c36   1994   94-11621

975.6'88 — dc20   cip

Front cover photo by Sandra Stambaugh. Copyright page: George Vanderbilt's bookplate.

Back cover (clockwise from top left): Biltmore's Shrub Garden, Italian Garden, Biltmore House from the Lagoon (by James Valentine), and Bass Pond bridge.

Printed in China

I never knew my great-grandfather, George Vanderbilt, but I cherish the memories of him that have been passed down through the family. I know, for example, his vision for Biltmore was one of a self-sufficient estate, where a home equipped with cutting-edge technology of the day would stand at the center of a carefully designed working farm and a beautiful park and woods. I know, too, that he loved to travel. He filled Biltmore House with the treasures he brought back from England, Italy, France, and Asia. And most of all, I know he took special pride in sharing his home with others. From the first day Biltmore was opened, on Christmas Eve in 1895, it was often host to family and friends — everyone from famous artists to neighborhood children.

Guests remain a central part of the Estate today. You keep alive the pleasure my great-grandfather took in entertaining and enable us to maintain his ideal of a private working estate that sustains itself and benefits the community. We appreciate your support as we embark upon new projects allowing us to remain self-sufficient and a leader in historic preservation through private enterprise.

I know my great-grandfather would be pleased that so many people continue to visit his home and perpetuate his dream. I hope, as you tour the Estate and extend your experience by a stay at the inn, that you enjoy yourself as thoroughly as the honored guests who have preceded you. And that you take home memories as precious as my own.

Welcome to Biltmore.

William A. V. Cecil, Jr.

FOREWORD

THE STORY OF
Biltmore™

Biltmore is a testament to the uncom-

promising ideals of an exceptional

man — George Washington Vanderbilt.

What began as his vision of a country

retreat became the largest private

residence in America and stands to

this day as a celebrated historic land-

mark. To visit Biltmore is to cross the

threshold into a world of hospitality,

beauty, and luxury that has remained

unchanged for more than a century

and is being preserved for many gener-

ations yet to come.

When George Washington Vanderbilt III welcomed family and friends to Biltmore Estate on Christmas Eve in 1895, his holiday celebration marked the formal opening of the most ambitious home ever conceived in America. For six years, an army of artisans had labored to create a country estate that would rival the great manors of Europe and embody the finest in architecture, landscape planning, and interior design. The results were astounding.

Boasting four acres of floor space, the 250-room mansion featured 33 family and guest bedrooms, 43 bathrooms, 65 fireplaces, three kitchens, and an indoor swimming pool. It was appointed with a priceless collection of furnishings and artworks and equipped with every conceivable amenity, from elevators to refrigerators. The surrounding grounds were equally impressive, encompassing 125,000 acres of forests, farms and a dairy, a 250-acre wooded park, five pleasure gardens, and 30 miles of macadamized roadways.

The youngest in a family renowned for building palatial homes, 33-year-old George Vanderbilt had outdone them all.

A FAMILY LEGACY

The Vanderbilts were not only one of the best-known families in America, but they were also among the oldest: Jan Aertsen van der Bilt had emigrated to this country from Holland around 1650. Although his descendants prospered as farmers on Staten Island, New York, they lived modestly; it was only during the lifetime of Cornelius Vanderbilt (1794–1877) that the family name became synonymous with extraordinary wealth.

Legend holds that Cornelius changed the family fortune at age 16 with a $100 loan from his mother. Strong willed and self-educated, the budding entrepreneur launched a ferry service across New York Bay, which he eventually parlayed into a fleet of more than 100 steamboats that traveled as far as Central America and Europe. Some 50 years later, the "Commodore," as he came to be called, earned his second fortune investing in railroads,

OPPOSITE: George Vanderbilt, seen in a turn-of-the-century photograph on display in the Tapestry Gallery, was only 33 years old when he opened Biltmore.

ABOVE: The Estate as it appeared in the late 1890s. It remains the largest private residence in America.

ABOVE: A patron of the arts and a collector of fine paintings, William Henry Vanderbilt commissioned *Going to the Opera* from the American artist Seymour Guy in 1873. William Henry is seated at the left and is surrounded by his wife, their eight children, and other family members. George Vanderbilt is the young boy seated in front of his father.

the fabled New York Central among them. He began the Vanderbilt tradition of philanthropy, contributing $1 million in 1873 to Central University, a Methodist school in Nashville; it was renamed Vanderbilt University.

The Commodore was the patriarch of a sizable family—including his wife of 53 years, Sophia, 13 children, 37 grandchildren, and 27 great-grandchildren. Upon his death the Commodore left most of his $100 million estate—a sum that made him the wealthiest industrialist of his time—to his eldest son, William Henry (1821–85). Although his father had once considered him unsuited for business, William Henry took over the family empire and eventually doubled his assets. He, too, was generous toward worthy causes, funding the Metropolitan Opera in 1883 and endowing the College of Physicians and Surgeons, now the Medical School of Columbia University.

The shrewd financier proved to be an equally astute collector, assembling more than 200 paintings. These were displayed in the 58-room mansion he built in 1881 at 640 Fifth Avenue—the largest and most splendid house in Manhattan at that time. Outfitted with all the latest conveniences, such as telephones and refrigeration, the house was exquisitely

THE VANDERBILT FAMILY

The Vanderbilts are a large family descended in America from Jan Aertsen van der Bilt, who emigrated from Holland around 1650. The first family member to gain prominence was Cornelius, known as the "Commodore," who married Sophia Johnson in 1813 (both, top row, at left). Their eldest son was William Henry, who in 1841 married Maria Louisa Kissam *(both, top row, at right)*. Their youngest child was George Washington, who wed Edith Stuyvesant Dresser in 1898 *(both, at right)*. They had one child, Cornelia Stuyvesant (below right), who married John Cecil in 1924. The younger of their two sons is William A.V. Cecil, shown with his wife, children, and grandchildren *(below)*.

ABOVE: George Vanderbilt around 1874.

BELOW LEFT: George's travel diary from 1880, when he sailed to Europe aboard the steamship Brittanic for a five-month tour of Italy, England, France, Switzerland, and Germany.

BELOW RIGHT: Mr. Vanderbilt (seated, rear) cruised along the canals of Venice in the 1890s; the Doge's Palace and the Piazza San Marco are in the background.

decorated with European furniture, tapestries, stained-glass windows, and countless art objects; it also had a glass-roofed stable courtyard so his beloved trotting horses could exercise without being exposed to the weather.

Only one of the eight children of William Henry and his wife, Maria Louisa (1821–96), was still living at home when the house was completed; the youngest, George, born in 1862. Quiet and intellectual, he had been greatly influenced by his father's cultural interests, starting his own collection of art and books at an early age; he even oversaw the design of his private quarters, including a library, in the new mansion. Significantly, George Vanderbilt would inherit the house and its contents after his mother's death.

Unlike his older brothers, however, Mr. Vanderbilt was little attracted to the family business. He preferred the world of learning and travel, taking his first trip to Europe at age 10 and journeying to Europe, Asia, and Africa many times throughout his adult life. It was while traveling in the mountains of North Carolina that Mr. Vanderbilt first glimpsed his destiny.

A VISION UNFOLDS

Asheville was a popular health resort in the late 19th century, when train service brought tourists into the southern Appalachians to enjoy the mineral springs, fresh air, and pleasant climate. When George Vanderbilt visited in 1888 with his mother, he was captivated by the rugged beauty of the rural region and found it the perfect setting for a new home.

He engaged two of the most distinguished designers of the 19th century to create this house: the architect Richard Morris Hunt (1828–95) and the landscape architect

Frederick Law Olmsted (1822–1903). Together they envisioned an estate—one that would serve not only as a showcase for Vanderbilt's cherished collections and a retreat for entertaining but also as a profitable, self-supporting business. They based these concepts on vast baronies in Europe, where country estates had endured for centuries preserving both family and national heritage. Other influences were the Vanderbilt tradition of extravagant homes and the 3,500-acre Vermont estate, Shelburne Farms, that Lila Vanderbilt and her husband, William Seward Webb, had created in 1886.

ABOVE: Biltmore Estate was the result of a collaboration among three talented men: Richard Morris Hunt (standing, second from left), George Washington Vanderbilt (standing, right), and Frederick Law Olmsted (sitting, center).

Taking the first step, Mr. Vanderbilt began purchasing parcels of land—which was both affordable and readily available in this area—eventually amassing 125,000 acres, including the 100,000-acre tract which became Pisgah Forest. He called his estate "Biltmore"—from Bildt, the Dutch town where his ancestors originated, and "more," an old English word for open, rolling land.

Mr. Vanderbilt had known both Hunt and Olmsted for several years; they collaborated on the Staten Island family mausoleum William Henry commissioned in 1884. Hunt, the first American to study at the prestigious Ecole des Beaux-Arts in Paris, was a favorite society architect. He became the unofficial family designer, creating Marble House and The Breakers in Newport, Rhode Island, and a mansion at 660 Fifth Avenue for one of George Vanderbilt's older brothers. Hunt was also responsible for many major public works, such as the main facade of the Metropolitan Museum of Art in New York, the Yorktown Monument in Virginia, and the pedestal for the Statue of Liberty.

Olmsted, who was trained in engineering and agriculture and was known as the founding father of American landscape architecture, had designed scores of parks, most notably New York's Central Park, the U.S. Capitol grounds, and the campus of Stanford University in California. An early conservationist, he also consulted in 1864 on the preservation of Yosemite Valley, which later became one of America's first national parks.

For these gifted professionals, Biltmore represented the pinnacle of their long careers. Together with George Vanderbilt they built not only an estate but also a close working relationship based on cooperation and respect.

BUILDING BEGINS

Construction of Biltmore got under way in 1889; it was a massive undertaking that included a mansion, gardens, farms, and woodlands.

The centerpiece was a four-story stone house with a 375-foot-long front facade—a monument rivalling the surrounding mountains in grandeur. Hunt modeled the architecture on the richly ornamented style of the French Renaissance and adapted elements, such as the stair tower and the steeply pitched roof, from three famous early 16th-century châteaux in the Loire Valley: Blois, Chenonceau, and Chambord.

The interiors, too, were inspired by European properties, such as the English country estates of Knole, Hatfield House, and Haddon Hall, which Hunt and his client had visited in 1889 while on a buying trip for furnishings. In turn-of-the-century fashion, Biltmore was to be decorated with custom-made pieces and an eclectic assortment of English, Continental, and American furniture and artworks in a range of period styles.

Biltmore was conceived as a masterwork of design and a marvel of modern technology. In addition to central heating, electricity, and a plumbing system that piped fresh water from a mountain reservoir several miles away, the House was equipped with fire alarms, mechanical refrigeration, and elevators.

Construction required hundreds of workers, from local laborers who earned 50 cents per day to skilled artisans and internationally known artists. The American sculptor Karl Bitter (1867–1915), a Hunt protégé, was hired to design elaborate works in stone, wood, and bronze. Another noted contributor was the Spanish architect Rafael Guastavino (1842–1908), who emigrated to America in the 1880s and quickly became known for the unique system for building tiled ceiling vaults that he had perfected.

Among the countless tons of materials used were limestone hauled 600 miles from Indiana and marble imported from Italy. Supplies were delivered via a three-mile-long

BELOW: Mr. Vanderbilt bought this photograph of the Château de Blois in 1889, during his trip to the Loire Valley with Hunt. The stair tower of the 16th-century French castle inspired the one at Biltmore, which spirals in the opposite direction.

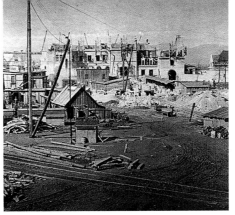

private rail spur laid between the depot in a neighboring village and the Estate. An on-site kiln produced some 32,000 bricks daily, and a woodworking factory processed oak and walnut for floors and paneling.

As the House was being built, work also progressed on the grounds. Because the tract had been overworked and the terrain was too "rough" for the extensive parkland George Vanderbilt originally desired, Olmsted devised a more practical plan. He recommended installing a 250-acre pleasure park and a series of gardens around the House, establishing farms along the fertile river bottoms, and replanting the rest of the property as commercial timber forest.

One of Olmsted's first projects was creating a nursery to supply the millions of plants needed for the grounds. In 1890 he hired as nursery superintendent Chauncey Beadle (1867–1950), a Canadian horticulturist trained at Ontario Agricultural College and Cornell University. Beadle remained on the Estate for 60 years, guiding Olmsted's plan to maturity. Gifford Pinchot (1865–1946) was engaged in 1891 to oversee renovation of the forest. An 1889 graduate of Yale University, Pinchot studied forestry at the Ecole Nationale Forestière in Nancy, France, and developed at Biltmore the first planned forestry program in America.

TOP LEFT: Biltmore House was located on a bluff high above the confluence of the French Broad and Swannanoa rivers. In 1889 the site was farmland.

TOP RIGHT: Building materials and work sheds covered the front court as construction proceeded. The rail line was installed to expedite delivery of supplies.

BOTTOM LEFT: Scaffolding surrounds the stair tower and entrance door.

BOTTOM RIGHT: Hundreds of masons, carpenters, and other artisans worked on Biltmore House over the course of six years. Seen here are members of the construction crew in 1893.

ESTATE LIFE

After six years of construction, Biltmore was opened on Christmas Eve 1895, when guests gathered to celebrate with a gaily trimmed tree, holiday feasts, and a coaching party. It was the first of many gala affairs on the Estate, which played host to such luminaries as novelists Edith Wharton and Henry James. Guests also came to relax and partake of a range of diversions, from tennis, archery, and croquet to picnicking, riding, and hunting; evenings brought concerts, parlor games, or perhaps dancing.

In addition to being used for entertaining, Biltmore was very much a home. It was here that George Vanderbilt started a family and pursued his interests in art, literature, and horticulture. He married Edith Stuyvesant Dresser (1873–1958) in June 1898 in Paris, and the couple came to live at the Estate that fall after honeymooning in Europe. Their only child, Cornelia (1900–76), was born and grew up at Biltmore.

The Vanderbilts were attended by a large staff, including domestic servants and stable hands, and were known as kind and generous employers. Besides paying good wages

FROM LEFT TO RIGHT: Guests could enjoy a range of entertainments, including going for a drive in a horse-drawn carriage, picnicking and hiking in the woodlands, or playing croquet on the lawn of the Italian Garden.

and providing comfortable living quarters, they held a Christmas party for the staff each year as a special measure of thanks, decorating an enormous tree with gifts for employees and their children.

As the new century progressed, Mr. Vanderbilt realized his dream of a productive estate. The farms yielded fruits, vegetables, grain crops, meat and dairy products, and honey from 100 beehives. The forest produced thousands of cords of firewood annually, which were sold along with lumber processed at Biltmore's own mill. And the 300-acre nursery, complete with greenhouses, cold frames, and seed beds, offered for sale five million plants—one of the most complete stocks in the country until it was destroyed by flood in 1916.

George and Edith Vanderbilt were committed to helping others. In 1889, Mr. Vanderbilt purchased the nearby town of Best, renaming it Biltmore Village. Between 1896 and 1902, under Mr. Vanderbilt's direction, the town grew to include a school, hospital, church, shops, and cottages. These rental cottages were complete with plumbing

BELOW LEFT: Estate employees lined the Approach Road in October 1898 to welcome newlyweds George and Edith Vanderbilt to Biltmore.

BOTTOM LEFT: Cornelia hosts her cousin John Brown at a tea party around 1905.

BELOW RIGHT: Mr. Vanderbilt shows off his daughter Cornelia, born in 1900.

BOTTOM RIGHT: Edith and Cornelia Vanderbilt lead a parade of carriages through Biltmore Village in 1906.

ABOVE: The Vanderbilts started three schools in the early 1900s: the School for Domestic Science (left), which taught housekeeping, Biltmore Estate Industries (right), which taught craft skills, and the Biltmore Parish Day School, an elementary school for local children.

and central heating, considered unusual amenities for the time. Mr. Vanderbilt also introduced innovative farming techniques to the rural region and championed the founding of the Biltmore Forest School in 1898—the first institute for scientific forestry in America.

In 1901, Edith Vanderbilt became involved with the Boys' and Girls' Club of All Souls Church. With her support, the club evolved into Biltmore Estate Industries, an apprenticeship program to teach traditional crafts such as woodworking and weaving; students sold their works to earn a living, and often made reproductions of Biltmore furnishings. Two years later, Mrs. Vanderbilt set up the School for Domestic Science, which trained young women in cooking, cleaning, and other housekeeping skills. Students in both programs learned essential skills to expand their job opportunities.

YEARS OF CHANGE

While the Vanderbilts owned several other residences, Mr. Vanderbilt was actively involved with the operation of Biltmore until his unexpected death in March 1914 following an emergency appendectomy in Washington, D.C. After his burial in the family mausoleum, in Staten Island, New York, Mrs. Vanderbilt returned to the Estate and

resumed her work in the community, becoming the first woman president of the state agricultural society, helping build a new hospital, and advocating literacy programs.

After a time, however, she found managing the large property to be overwhelming and began consolidating her interests. Honoring her husband's wish to preserve Pisgah Forest for the public, she sold nearly 87,000 acres to the federal government in 1915, creating the nucleus of Pisgah National Forest. She sold Biltmore Estate Industries in 1917 and Biltmore Village in 1921; by the late 1920s, the Estate comprised about 11,000 acres (it is currently 8,000 acres).

In 1925, Edith married Senator Peter G. Gerry; the couple maintained homes in Providence, Rhode Island, Washington, D.C., and Asheville. Cornelia continued to live at Biltmore; she had been married the year before at All Souls Church in Biltmore Village to the Honorable John Francis Amherst Cecil (1890–1954), a descendant of William Cecil (1520–98), Lord Burghley, who was Lord High Treasurer to Queen Elizabeth I. Their two sons, George Henry Vanderbilt Cecil and William Amherst Vanderbilt Cecil, were born on the Estate in 1925 and 1928, respectively.

ABOVE LEFTT: All Souls Church under construction in Biltmore Village.

ABOVE RIGHT: The first woman president of the North Carolina Agricultural Society, Edith Vanderbilt takes the wheel of a tractor as Cornelia looks on.

BELOW: Cornelia and John Cecil with their first child, George. Both of their sons were born at Biltmore Estate.

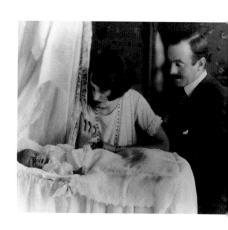

The Cecils opened the Estate to the public for the first time in March 1930 in response to a request by the city of Asheville, which hoped to revitalize the Depression-era economy with tourism, and to generate funds to maintain the estate. During World War II, when it was believed the capital was at risk of air attack, priceless artworks from the National Gallery of Art were sent to Biltmore House for safekeeping. During this time the Biltmore dairy grew into a thriving enterprise that provided both employment and top-quality products.

BILTMORE TODAY

In 1960, William Cecil left a banking career in New York City and Washington, D.C., to join his brother in managing Biltmore, which they inherited under the terms of a trust. His goal was not only to return the historic site to its turn-of-the-century splendor but also to perpetuate his grandfather's ideal of self-sufficiency.

ABOVE: Conservators spend many hours restoring items in the collection, such as this gilded wooden sconce in the Second Floor Living Hall.

Under Mr. Cecil's stewardship, more than 50 rooms with thousands of original objects were opened to the public. He began an ongoing preservation program which made it possible to experience the Estate as it was during the Vanderbilts' residence. Mrs. Vanderbilt's Bedroom, for instance, was restored in 1990 using reproductions of the original French fabrics woven on the same looms used a century earlier. Mr. Cecil's commitment to preservation also entailed creating an in-house conservation team of textile and furniture conservators. A landmark project was conservation of eight 16th-century tapestries which took 17 years to complete.

Mr. Cecil also brought an innovative business approach to the management of Biltmore as a private, for-profit, family-owned enterprise. After the dairy, under the leadership of George Cecil, became a separate business in 1979, the dairy barn was remodeled for use as a winery, which has become the most visited winery in America. Angus and

Limousin beef cattle were introduced in the farm operation, and a breeding program produced several champions. Special events, including *Christmas at Biltmore*, *Candlelight
Christmas Evenings*, and *Festival of Flowers*, were introduced to encourage guest visitation.

In 1995, William Cecil celebrated the 100th anniversary of Biltmore's completion with
a banquet and ball in Biltmore House for family, friends, and many estate employees. Mr.
Cecil announced his retirement, passing leadership to his son William A.V. Cecil, Jr., who
assumed the role of President and CEO of The Biltmore Company. Another milestone
occurred in 2001 with the opening of the Inn on Biltmore Estate, the first lodging on
estate grounds. In 2004, River Bend Farm, which includes the original horse barn, farmyard, and market garden, was restored and opened to the public. By 2007, employment
rose to more than 1,700, making Biltmore one of the region's largest employers.

Most importantly, Biltmore today maintains the tradition of hospitality engendered by
its founder, welcoming more than one million guests each year to its celebrated house,
gardens, winery, and farm. Named a National Historic Landmark in 1963, Biltmore continues to attract visitors and to inspire all who see it just as it has since 1895.

ABOVE: Outside the Library, the Loggia glows as the sun sets over the Deer Park.

BILTMORE™
House

No residence in America offers a more authentic, original, and inspiring view of life at the end of the 1800s than Biltmore House. Faithfully preserved and filled with thousands of original furnishings, its rooms suggest that the Vanderbilts, their friends, and employees are still at home. From opulent living quarters enjoyed by family and friends to the "downstairs" domain of the domestic staff, the House presents a detailed portrait of life on a great 19th-century country estate.

*O*n the main floor of Biltmore are the public rooms in which the Vanderbilts lived as a family and entertained their guests. Arranged around a light-filled garden court are an entry hall, a billiard room, and several dining and sitting areas; set off by itself is an expansive library, a quiet retreat for study or solitude. The decor throughout is richly elegant, reflecting the traditions of European country estates.

ENTRANCE HALL

With its soaring limestone arches and polished marble floor, the Entrance Hall is an impressive introduction to Biltmore House. Its focal point is a massive oak table designed by Richard Howland Hunt, which displays a group of bronzes by renowned French artist Antoine-Louis Barye (1796–1875). Inspired by the 16th-century Italian epic poem Orlando Furioso, the center sculpture portrays the hero, Roger, rescuing his love, Angelique, on a mythical creature called the Hippogriff. The flanking candelabra are modeled with figures of Roman goddesses Juno, Minerva, and Venus.

WINTER GARDEN

Glass-roofed garden rooms were considered quite stylish in the Victorian era, providing a place to relax or entertain amid an indoor "jungle" of exotic plants. Rattan and bamboo furniture such as this suite bought by Mr. Vanderbilt in France was fashionable for garden use. The central element of this indoor garden setting is a marble and bronze fountain sculpture, *Boy Stealing Geese*, by Karl Bitter, a Viennese artist who emigrated to America in 1889.

The adjoining corridor features tiled ceiling vaults designed by the Spanish architect Rafael Guastavino. On the walls are plaster copies of sections of the Elgin Marbles, crafted in the 1890s by French artist Eugene Arrondelle. The originals once adorned the Parthenon in Athens and are now housed in the British Museum.

ABOVE: Preserved in the pages of the Nonsense Book, a type of scrapbook for Biltmore's guests, is a sketch drawn in 1902 of Karl Bitter's bronze figures.

RIGHT: Cornelia Vanderbilt and John Cecil held their wedding breakfast by the fountain in 1924.

OPPOSITE: At Christmastime the palms, ficus, and other tropical plants in the Winter Garden are enhanced by colorful poinsettias.

BILLIARD ROOM

Part of a series of rooms known as the Bachelors' Wing, the Billiard Room provided a retreat for the Vanderbilts' male guests. (Concealed doors on either side of the fireplace lead to other rooms in the wing.) Although female guests were welcome, the room was primarily a place where men could enjoy each other's company and indulge in billiards, played on the carom table (with no pockets), or pool, played on the pool table (with six pockets). Both games became so popular by the late 18th century that special rooms like this began to appear in country homes. Biltmore's one-of-a-kind tables were custom built by the manufacturer Brunswick-Balke-Collender Co.

The Billiard Room resembles exclusive gentlemen's social clubs of the age, with rich oak paneling, an ornamental plaster ceiling, and deep-hued Oriental carpets. Equally masculine are the leather settees and armchairs made in London in 1895; the pieces are reproductions of 17th-century furniture from Knole, an English estate that Mr. Vanderbilt and Hunt visited in 1889.

Displayed around the room are examples from Mr. Vanderbilt's print collection. Many of the works are based on paintings by the British artists Sir Joshua Reynolds (1723–92), George Stubbs (1724–1806), and Sir Edwin Landseer (1802–73).

OPPOSITE: Illuminated by wrought-iron light fixtures made especially for the room, the American billiard tables are each topped with three slabs of slate weighing about 900 pounds. Many of the 24 cue sticks, stored in their original oak stands, are inlaid with ivory and mother-of-pearl.

PRINTS

Mr. Vanderbilt was an avid collector of prints, acquiring about 1,600 etchings, woodcuts, aquatints, photogravures, and other printed works throughout his life. Examples from the collection, which includes sporting, architecture, landscape, still-life, and portrait prints, are (from above left) *Rhinoceros*, a 1515 woodcut by Albrecht Dürer; a likeness of Cardinal Richelieu engraved in 1657 by Robert Nanteuil; and *Chartres: Street Scene and Cathedral*, an 1882 etching by Axel Haig.

ABOVE: Karl Bitter is shown with the oak frieze he carved in 1897 for the organ loft.

BELOW: The figures depict characters from *Tannhäuser*, an opera by the 19th-century German composer Richard Wagner.

OPPOSITE: Although massive in proportion, the Banquet Hall has perfect acoustics: two people sitting at opposite ends of the dining table could converse without having to raise their voices.

BANQUET HALL

As imposing as a great hall in a medieval castle, the Banquet Hall is the largest room in the House, measuring 72 feet long by 42 feet wide with a 70-foot-high barrel-vaulted ceiling. It was in this baronial space that the Vanderbilts dined, whether at a table set for two or 32. It was also in this room that they held their annual Christmas festivities—a tradition that continues to this day.

Because of the room's vast dimensions, Hunt and his son Richard Howland Hunt designed special furniture for it, including two built-in gilt-trimmed throne chairs, an oak dining table, and 67 chairs. The architect also created a suitable setting for the five Flemish tapestries that Mr. Vanderbilt is thought to have purchased in Paris in 1887. These intricate textiles, woven of silk, wool, and metallic thread between 1546 and 1553, are part of an original set of seven portraying the story from Roman mythology of Venus (goddess of love); her paramour, Mars (god of war); and her jealous husband, Vulcan (god of fire).

The triple fireplace, flanked with armor dating from the 1400s to 1800s, features on its overmantel a high-relief panel entitled *The Return from the Chase*. It was carved by Karl Bitter, who was also responsible for the oak frieze on the organ gallery. Although an instrument was not originally installed, an organ from the period has been restored and placed in the room. Below the gallery is a built-in sideboard showcasing a collection of 18th- and 19th-century brass and copper vessels from Holland, France, and Spain.

The pennants hanging in the room include the Biltmore Estate service flag, commemorating staff members who fought in World War I, and replicas of flags from the American Revolution and the 13 original colonies. Those hanging above the fireplace represent countries in power when Christopher Columbus sailed to North America; the 400th anniversary of his second voyage was celebrated in 1893 by the World's Columbian Exposition in Chicago, which Mr. Vanderbilt visited.

BREAKFAST ROOM

Designed on a more intimate scale than the Banquet Hall, this room was intended for less formal dining at breakfast and luncheon. Nevertheless, the room is elegant, with Italian marble wainscoting and door trim, a tooled-leather wall covering, and a fireplace surround of Wedgwood-style jasperware tiles. The ornate plasterwork ceiling is highlighted with a gold-tinted glaze and features heavy pendants that terminate in tiny acorns—one of the symbols in the Vanderbilt family crest.

No finery was spared in setting the dining table, spread with damask linens probably woven in Ireland and embroidered in Paris. Seated on gilt-legged chairs with cut-velvet upholstery, diners were served their meals on gold-trimmed porcelain dinnerware made by Minton, the noted Staffordshire ceramics manufacturer. And, they drank from crystal glasses—etched with Vanderbilt monograms—produced by Baccarat of France and Thomas Webb and Sons of England.

Among the family portraits in this room are likenesses of Mr. Vanderbilt's father, William Henry, located above the display case, and of his mother, Maria Louisa, to the right of the fireplace. There are two paintings of his grandfather, Cornelius: the circa 1839 portrait to the left of the fireplace shows him as a successful businessman (appropriately, for a mariner, holding a spyglass) and the circa 1876 portrait above the Banquet Hall door depicts him as the wealthiest man in America.

ABOVE: Each of the hundreds of pieces in the family table service bears a monogram; this tureen is marked with "CSV" for Cornelia Stuyvesant Vanderbilt.

OPPOSITE: As part of the restoration of the Breakfast Room in 1993, the seating furniture was reupholstered and the draperies replaced using 350 yards of silk cut velvet matched to the original pattern. The fabric was woven by Tassinari & Chatel of Lyons, France—the same textile firm that filled Mr. Vanderbilt's order in the 1890s.

OPPOSITE: The Salon boasts one of the many interesting ceiling treatments used throughout the House. It is draped with wool brocade tenting, a feature perhaps inspired by the Victorian passion for exotic Asian and Moorish decorating styles.

SALON

Though clearly identified on Richard Morris Hunt's architectural floor plans as "Salon," this room remained unfinished during Mr. Vanderbilt's residence. Just why it was not completed is still a mystery. In the French tradition in which salons originated, the salon was a room most often inhabited by the hostess of the house and her female guests. There they would engage in polite conversation, with literature, art, and music often being topics of discussion.

Today the Salon is decorated as it might have been, using furnishings original to the Biltmore collection. The decor features graceful furniture in the French Louis XV style, including an intricately inlaid 18th-century commode or chest of drawers. The room is also a showcase for prints by Albrecht Dürer (1471–1528), the noted German artist, and 19th-century prints of châteaux in the Loire Valley.

Reflecting Mr. Vanderbilt's interest in the Napoleonic era is the Empire walnut game table and ivory chess pieces owned and used by Napoleon Bonaparte during his exile on St. Helena island between 1815 and 1821. After the deposed emperor's death, his heart was placed in a silver urn on the table before being put into his coffin.

GAMES

At Biltmore, family and guests had a choice of pleasant pastimes, from cribbage to checkers. Card games, such as whist and euchre, were played with gaily decorated decks (bottom). Chess players used a 19th-century game table and ivory pieces (above left) originally owned by Napoleon Bonaparte. Gentlemen gambled with poker chips and an American-made walnut roulette wheel (above right). Mah-jongg was a popular Chinese game using tiles, and Biltmore's set (above)—made in Hong Kong—is located in the Second Floor Living Hall.

ABOVE: The figure of St. Matthew is part of a set portraying the 12 apostles that was produced by the Meissen porcelain factory in the mid 1700s. The base is marked with the Austrian imperial crest; the Biltmore sculptures are based on statuary found in a Roman basilica.

BELOW: A detail from the monumental *Triumphal Arch*, designed by Albrecht Dürer and others. Comprising 192 separately printed blocks, the work arrived at Biltmore just before Christmas 1895, shipped by train in three boxes.

OPPOSITE: Unfinished during Mr. Vanderbilt's lifetime, the Music Room contains a Steinway piano—played by Van Cliburn during his visit to the Estate in 1961—and an elaborately carved and gilded 18th-century music stand.

MUSIC ROOM

Plans for Biltmore indicate that a music room was intended for this location, although it remained unfinished for 81 years. What had been an empty space with bare brick walls was completed and opened in 1976. The room is decorated to reflect the French Renaissance style and includes wall paneling carved of red oak harvested from Biltmore's forest and polychrome painting on the boxed ceiling beams.

The room was also designed to display several treasures. The fireplace mantel, designed by Hunt and carved with Albrecht Dürer's initials and life dates, was found below the stables prior to installation in the Music Room. Above it hangs a late 18th-century printing of the woodcut known as the *Triumphal Arch*, which Holy Roman Emperor Maximilian I (1459–1519) commissioned from Dürer and others around 1515. Measuring about 10 feet tall by 10 feet wide, the work depicts military and political events, references to the emperor's prowess as a hunter and linguist, and a family tree with mythological and human characters.

On the shelves beside the print is a rare collection of 12 apostle figures and 12 candlesticks. Based on statuary in the Basilica of St. John Lateran in Rome, the gilt-trimmed porcelain sculptures are the work of Johann Joachim Kändler (1706–75), master modeler at the Meissen factory near Dresden. The pieces came from several different sets made between 1735 and 1741 for Empresses Amalia and Maria Theresa of the Austrian Hapsburgs.

TAPESTRY GALLERY

Opening off the Entrance Hall, this 90-foot-long room served as a sitting area. The space was also designed to display three silk-and-wool tapestries woven in Brussels around 1530. Part of an original set of seven known as *The Triumph of the Seven Virtues*, the pieces are distinguished by richly detailed pictorial designs that personify Prudence, Faith, and Charity and incorporate biblical, mythological, and historical images.

Other notable furnishings include three 19th-century Persian rugs—examples of the several hundred Eastern carpets Mr. Vanderbilt acquired on his trips to Europe. In 1889, for instance, he bought 300 carpets at one time from a single London dealer. Not all the furniture, however, came from abroad. The two gateleg tables with spiral-twist legs were probably produced by Biltmore Estate Industries, the handicraft program founded by the Vanderbilts in 1901.

Three family portraits hang on the paneled wall to the Library. Over the door is the likeness of George Vanderbilt, painted in 1895, and to the left is that of his mother, Maria Louisa Kissam Vanderbilt, painted around 1888. Both are the work of John Singer Sargent (1856–1925), one of the most celebrated society portraitists of his time. On the right is Edith Vanderbilt, painted in 1911 by Giovanni Boldini (1842–1931), an Italian artist who enjoyed an international reputation at the turn of the century. On the opposite wall, near the entrance hall, is another portrait of Edith Vanderbilt. Entitled *Ivory and Gold*, it was painted in 1902 by James Abbott McNeill Whistler (1834–1903), the famous expatriate American artist.

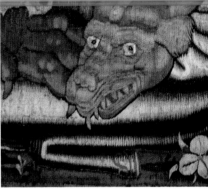

OPPOSITE: Providing a colorful setting for three 16th-century Flemish tapestries are stenciled ceiling beams and painted limestone fireplace hoods modeled after those in the Château de Pierrefonds near Compiègne, France.

ABOVE: One of three fearsome serpent heads, part of the complex design of the *Triumph of Prudence* tapestry, is shown in detail.

LIBRARY

Of all the rooms in Biltmore House, the Library best reflects Mr. Vanderbilt's intellect and personality. An avid reader and book lover from childhood, George Vanderbilt began acquiring books by age 11. He amassed a collection of more than 23,000 volumes, about 10,000 of which are housed in the Library's walnut stacks. His interests were wide-ranging, as evidenced by books on everything from architecture to agriculture.

Mr. Vanderbilt enjoyed sharing his library with guests. A passage behind the mantel leads to the second floor, which provided easy access for guests to select volumes for bedtime reading. (Even so, Henry James, the noted American author who visited Biltmore in 1905, complained that his bedroom was at least half a mile away from the "mile-long library.")

Among the striking features of the room is a dramatic ceiling painting—*The Chariot of Aurora*, by the Venetian artist Giovanni Antonio Pellegrini (1675–1741). Originally located in the ballroom of the Pisani Palace in Venice, the work comprises 13 separate canvases and measures about 64 feet long by 32 feet wide.

Equally impressive are the black marble fireplace surround and the walnut overmantel. Baroque-style carvings and two female figures carved by Bitter flank the 17th-century French tapestry. In 1999–2000, upholstery, drapery fabric, and trims were painstakingly reproduced to restore the Library to its original appearance.

OPPOSITE: Stocked with books dating as early as 1561, the Library was a source of both recreation and information for its scholarly owner.

LEFT: In this circa 1898 photograph, Cedric, one of the family's St. Bernards, rests in front of an ornate slant-front book rack designed by Hunt.

BELOW: Making the room appear open to the sky, the ceiling painting represents dawn. It is one of the most important canvases by Pellegrini extant, as many of his works were destroyed in the world wars.

*W*hereas the First Floor housed the grand public rooms, the second story was home to the Vanderbilts' private quarters and a series of guest suites. The floor is organized around a central sitting area where men and women could socialize, read, write letters, and play games. This and two other upper floors were reached by either a staircase or an Otis elevator, which traveled 100 feet per minute and was the first passenger elevator in Asheville.

LOUIS XVI ROOM

One of 31 guest rooms at Biltmore—needed to accommodate the Vanderbilts' large house parties—the Louis XVI Room exemplifies the rage for French decorating styles in the late 19th century. The room is characterized by its oval shape and its location above the main entrance to Biltmore House.

Decorated in neoclassical Louis XVI style—popular in the third quarter of the 18th century—the room is named for the King of France at that time. The style is represented by delicate column-shaped furniture legs, floral swags, and other classical Greek and Roman motifs.

Reflecting this style are the French-made chaise lounge, side chairs, and center table—Louis XVI-style pieces with slender, reeded legs and delicate swag or scroll motifs. Red damask upholstery and wall covering, exact reproductions of the original, and lightly patterned Aubusson carpets contribute to the refined look.

Pauline Merrill, Edith Vanderbilt's sister, described in a letter her experience while staying in this room as a guest in 1905. "*I breakfast in my room which is oval shape ... the walls hung in old crimson brocade & all the furniture & decorations Louis XVI ...*"

SECOND FLOOR LIVING HALL

The Living Hall was an area where occupants of the Second Floor guest rooms, along with family members, could mingle before meals or spend a lazy afternoon reading or chatting. Upholstered furniture in intimate groupings invited conversation, while a handsome Boulle-style desk offered a perfect place for letter writing.

Today the room serves as a gallery for several important paintings. In prominent positions on the north wall are full-length portraits of the two architects who helped translate Mr. Vanderbilt's vision for the Estate into reality. On the right is a portrait of Frederick Law Olmsted; the landscape designer is fittingly shown in a woodland setting beside a blossoming rhododendron. On the left is a portrait of Richard Morris Hunt, who is posed in front of the outside stair tower (although the weather was so chilly when the portrait was made that he actually stood indoors by a fireplace). Both were painted by John Singer Sargent, who came to Biltmore in May 1895 to capture these men on canvas. Between them hangs *The Waltz* by Anders Zorn (1860–1920), the respected Swedish artist; Mr. Vanderbilt purchased the painting in 1893 at the World's Columbian Exposition in Chicago, where it was on exhibit.

Family portraits include a likeness of Cornelia Vanderbilt Cecil, painted in the 1920s by the Russian artist Nikol Schattenstein (1877–1955). The group portrait at the east end is of the William Cecil family, painted by the prominent New York artist and Asheville native Stone Roberts (1951–). At the opposite end hangs *Going to the Opera*, a family portrait depicting the William Henry Vanderbilt family in 1873, by the American painter Seymour Guy (1824–75); 11-year-old George Vanderbilt is seated at the table.

OPPOSITE: The two tones of brown on the walls of the Living Hall are terra cotta and coffee brown. Through paint analysis these colors were carefully chosen to match the originals. This color scheme is found throughout the House in family and guest areas.

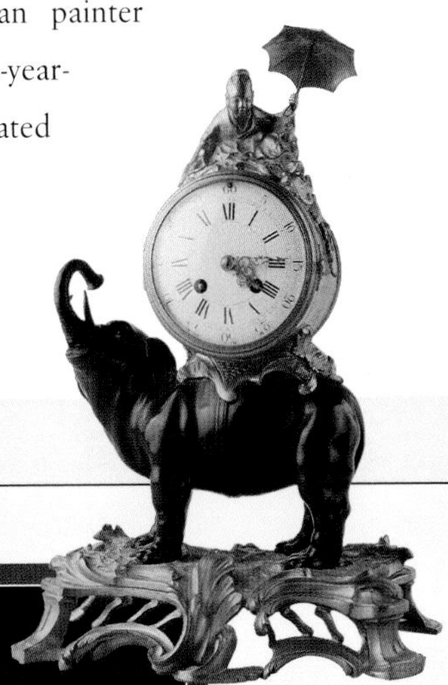

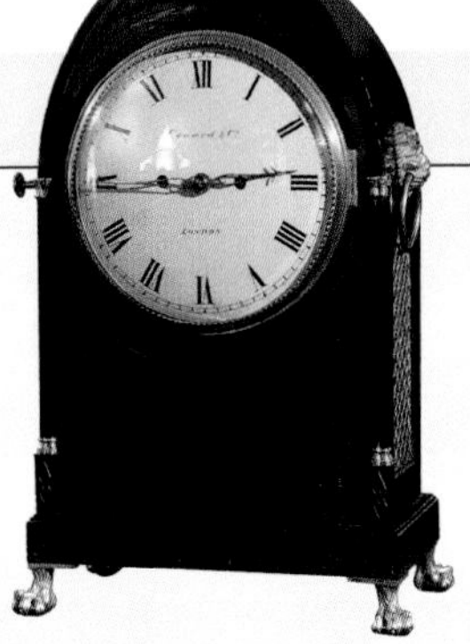

CLOCKS

Among the most intricate and varied objects at Biltmore are the clocks—from the tall-case clock in the Entrance Hall to the massive tower clock on the Stable to the mirror-mounted cartel clock in the Louis XVI Room. The 19 timepieces displayed from the collection range from the mid 17th century to the early 20th century and were made primarily in England and France. Shown here are a gilt-and-bronze statue clock (top right) with works by Japy Frères from around 1870, an arch-top bracket clock (far right) by Coward and Company circa 1780, and an inverted basket-top bracket clock (bottom right) made by Edmund Card in the late 1600s.

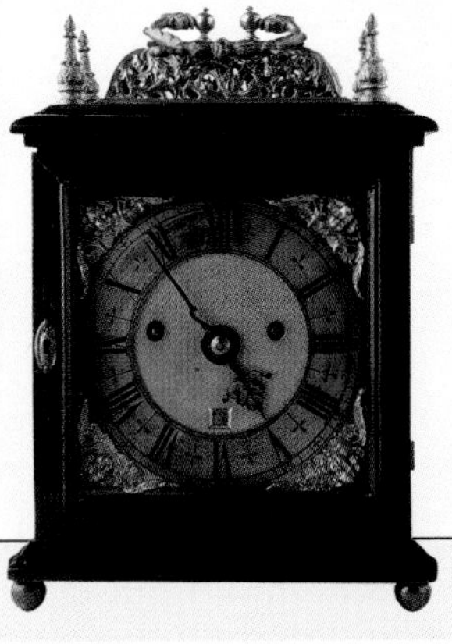

TOP LEFT: No detail in the bedroom was overlooked: the elaborate brass door latch was hand cast with floral and figural elements.

TOP RIGHT: Mr. Vanderbilt's bathroom, plumbed with hot and cold running water, features a paw-footed tub.

RIGHT: The bronze bust of Mr. Vanderbilt was created by the Scottish artist Mary Grant in 1889; it is displayed in the Library.

OPPOSITE: Befitting the head of the household is this dignified room, with deep ceiling moldings and a gilded wall covering. The furniture is a mixture of Baroque-style pieces from the 17th and 19th centuries. Mr. Vanderbilt's bed is a fine example of the intricate turned and carved walnut furniture produced in 17th-century Portugal.

MR. VANDERBILT'S BEDROOM

The owner of Biltmore was a man accustomed to the best, and he settled for nothing less in siting and furnishing his bedroom. It is located in the southwest corner of the House, where he could enjoy a commanding view of his property—from the wooded Deer Park below to Mount Pisgah, 17 miles in the distance. The room is filled with heavily carved and turned walnut pieces, including a dressing table, chaise lounge, and chairs designed by Hunt and inspired by the grand Baroque style.

Mr. Vanderbilt surrounded himself with the art objects he loved, such as fine engravings by 16th- and 17th-century artists from Germany and Holland and bronze sculptures from 19th-century France.

Through the door beside the bed is Mr. Vanderbilt's bath—another example of his fine appointments. The full-length mirror reflects his marble bathtub. Even though indoor plumbing was found in affluent homes as early as the 1830s, fully equipped bathrooms—with a toilet, sink, and bath or shower—were still uncommon in the 1890s. Rarer still was hot water available instantly at the turn of the tap, provided by two water heaters in the sub-basement, once fueled by coke, a coal by-product, but converted to electricity.

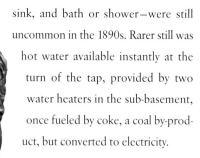

OAK SITTING ROOM

Connecting Mr. and Mrs. Vanderbilt's private quarters, this well-appointed room was used as a private sitting area for the couple. The ornate architectural detailing recalls the Jacobean splendor of the Great Hall at Hatfield House, a 17th-century English estate that Mr. Vanderbilt visited with Hunt during their trip to Europe in 1889. The plaster ceiling is webbed with intricate strapwork, the cornice frieze is marked with repeating coats of arms, and the walls are clad with exquisitely carved oak paneling.

The setting is complemented by the stately furnishings, which include several remarkable case pieces. In the corner is a carved ebony cabinet-on-stand made in Paris in the 1600s with parquetry doors that open to reveal a classically inspired architectural scene. Resembling a miniature loggia, it is decorated with a patterned floor, marbleized columns, and gilt-trimmed statuary overlooking a trompe-l'oeil landscape painting.

The room also features two portraits by Sargent. On the right, in a black dress, is *Mrs. Walter Rathbone Bacon*, a cousin and close friend of Mr. Vanderbilt's; on the left is *Mrs. Benjamin Kissam*, his aunt.

BRONZES

Of the more than 40 bronze sculptures on display at Biltmore, about half are pieces created by *les Animaliers*—a 19th-century French school of art so called because its adherents specialized in naturalistic depictions of animals. The most well-known of the group was Antoine-Louis Barye, who is considered one of the finest animal sculptors in history. Mr. Vanderbilt had seen Barye's work in Paris and acquired a number of his sculptures, including the striking *Hippogriff* seen in the Entrance Hall. Throughout the House are also pieces by Pierre-Jules Mène, whose stag (above left) exemplifies the artist's skill in portraying a moment of an animal's life in the wild; August Nicholas Cain, who crafted these candelabra (left) ornamented with bird nests; and Jean-François-Théodore Gechter, who was known for his horse figures, such as this horse spooked by a snake (below).

MRS. VANDERBILT'S BEDROOM

This graceful, feminine room was designed as a counterpart to Mr. Vanderbilt's Bedroom. It was decorated in 1897–98 in preparation for Mr. Vanderbilt's upcoming wedding. After his marriage, it became the private quarters of Edith Stuyvesant Dresser Vanderbilt.

Like her husband, Edith Vanderbilt was a member of a prominent family. Among her ancestors were Peter Stuyvesant, the first governor of Dutch colonial New York in the mid 17th century, and several respected senators, judges, and mayors. Orphaned at the age of ten, Edith Dresser and her sisters were raised by their maternal grandmother in Newport, Rhode Island. According to contemporary accounts, she was considered "a very charming young lady" and "the perfection of hostesses."

Her courtship with George Vanderbilt began in Paris in 1897; they had already known one another for several years. Engaged in April 1898, the couple wed in June in a simple ceremony, attended by 150 family members and friends, at the American Cathedral in Paris.

When they arrived at the Estate in October, after their honeymoon in Europe, Mrs. Vanderbilt saw her room just as it appears today. The oval-shaped space is decorated in the Louis XV style, which originated in France around 1725 and remained popular with Americans in the late 1800s. The room incorporates such hallmarks of this luxurious style as silk wall covering, fancily trimmed mirrors, Savonnerie carpets, and cut-velvet draperies on the windows and bed. The two marble-topped commodes are French period pieces; the chairs and chaise are in the Louis XV style, typified by white frames, carved floral motifs, and curving profiles. Complementing the look is a collection of French and German prints from the 18th century and a Louis XV clock elaborately embellished with porcelain figurines and flowers, believed to be Phillipe Barat's masterpiece, earning him entry into the French Clockmaker's guild in 1764.

OPPOSITE: The sumptuous cut velvet used for the draperies and upholstery in Mrs. Vanderbilt's Bedroom is a duplicate of the original fabric. It was woven for the restoration of the room in 1990 by Tassinari & Chatel, which retained the loom pattern from which the material had been made a century ago.

LEFT: A charming, fashionable woman, Mrs. Vanderbilt was the gracious hostess of Biltmore.

BELOW: Mrs. Vanderbilt was a devoted mother to her only daughter, Cornelia, seen here around age 5, who often accompanied her on weekly visits to families living on the Estate.

OPPOSITE: The satinwood tester bed in the Sheraton Room is elegantly draped with peach silk hangings and painted with bows, cherubs, and garlands. The piece is similar to a plate in Thomas Sheraton's first pattern book, *The Cabinet-Maker and Upholsterer's Drawing Book*, published between 1791 and 1794. The Biltmore House Library contains an original copy of this volume.

SHERATON ROOM

This elegant, sophisticated room is named for one of the foremost English furniture designers, Thomas Sheraton (1751–1806). His furniture designs, published in three widely read pattern books, were influential in the development of neoclassical decorating styles at the turn of the 19th century.

It would have been popular at the time to use classical wall coverings and fabrics in muted tones, as seen here in the wallpaper, bed hangings, and window draperies.

The English satinwood and mahogany furniture pieces in the Sheraton style—including a double desk, square-back sofa, and nightstand—are typically light and delicate, with tapered legs and graceful silhouettes.

Over the fireplace is a portrait of George Vanderbilt with siblings Frederick and Lila as children; George, the dark-haired boy on the left, would have been five years old when he sat for the artist Jacob H. Lazarus (1822–91) in 1867. On the other side of the doorway is a Currier & Ives print depicting William Henry Vanderbilt racing his famous trotters, Aldine and Maud S. (the latter bought for $20,000 in 1878).

CHIPPENDALE ROOM

Like the Sheraton Room, this guest room reflects the popularity of an important English furniture maker. Thomas Chippendale (1718–79) was the first to bring out a pattern book devoted entirely to furniture. In *The Gentleman and Cabinet-Maker's Director*, published in 1754, he presented a range of elaborate designs adapted from the Louis XV style and thereby influenced the fashion for fancy interiors.

Exemplifying the Chippendale style are the tester bed and seating furniture, which were made in 18th- and 19th-century England. These mahogany pieces include such typical stylistic elements as curved cabriole legs, hairy-paw feet, and carved leaf and shell motifs. Also in keeping with the period is the use of coordinating wallpaper and fabrics.

OLD ENGLISH ROOM

Decorated in the Jacobean style, this room provides an appropriate setting for the upholstered furniture, reproductions of 17th-century originals at Knole in Kent, England.

The designs feature mechanical parts adjusted by ratchets, allowing the sofa, for example, to be converted into a daybed.

On display are several Cecil family portraits which came into the collection after Cornelia Vanderbilt married the Honorable John Francis Amherst Cecil in 1924. Over the mantel is the Great Lord Burghley, William Cecil; above the oak chest are his grandchildren William and Frances, painted in 1599 by the Italian artist Frederico Zuccaro (1543–1609). Between the two is John Cecil, a direct descendant of William Cecil, Lord Burghley.

ABOVE LEFT: Among the family likenesses in the 17th-century-style Old English Room are William and Frances Cecil (above) and Lord Burghley (left), who was a principal minister to Queen Elizabeth I between 1558 and his death in 1598. The latter portrait was finished in 1589 by the Flemish painter Marcus Gheeraerts the Younger (1561–1636), a favorite artist of English royalty.

*L*ike the Second Floor, the Third Floor features a number of spacious guest rooms—each one decorated in a different style, as was fashionable in the late 19th century—and also includes a centrally located sitting area. The rooms here were removed from the noise and bustle of the First Floor and occupied by guests whose calling cards could be posted on each door—lest visitors lose their way among the many bedrooms on this level.

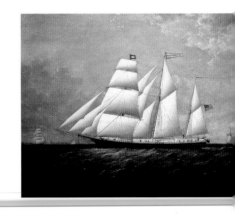

THIRD FLOOR LIVING HALL

This room, restored in 2002, served as a sitting area and upstairs library for guests staying on the third floor. They could take tea, match wits over parlor games, curl up with a book, or listen to the reproducing piano.

George Vanderbilt inherited the elaborately carved display cabinets from his father. Made by Herter Brothers of New York, they were originally used in the dining room of William H. Vanderbilt's Fifth Avenue home. It is believed that George Vanderbilt contracted William Baumgarten & Co. around 1905 to reconstruct the cabinets into free-standing furniture for Biltmore House. Three library tables and three open bookcases in the room feature the same Renaissance Revival motifs.

Many decorative objects in the room came from the large art collection of Vanderbilt's father. These include the Satsuma garniture set of two vases and a pail painted with realistic insects, a ship's portrait painting of the merchant vessel *William H. Vanderbilt*, and a bronze figure *Jean-Louis Messonier* by Vicenzo Gemito (1852–1929). Messonier was one of William H. Vanderbilt's favorite artists.

OPPOSITE: The library tables and open bookcases feature classical pilasters with Corinthian columns, acanthus leaves, and floral swags.

ABOVE: This portrait of the merchant vessel *William H. Vanderbilt* was originally part of the Fifth Avenue art collection of George Vanderbilt's father, William Henry Vanderbilt.

BELOW: During a 1892 trip to Japan, Vanderbilt purchased these 16th-and 17th-century Samurai swords.

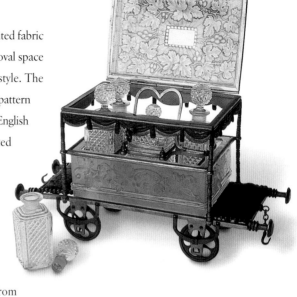

RIGHT: This diminutive railcar, complete with couplers and curtains, was made by the French *cristallerie* Baccarat around 1890 as a carriage for perfume flasks; the cushions at each end were designed for storing hat pins.

BELOW: Crafted in France in the 19th century, this ornate miniature furniture—measuring only four inches tall—is hand painted with pastoral scenes.

SOUTH TOWER ROOM

Pastel colors and dainty floral-printed fabric mark the South Tower Room, a large, oval space decorated in a subdued neo-classical style. The striated wallpaper was adapted from a pattern by William Morris (1834–96), a leading English proponent of "aesthetic" handcrafted design, and is complemented by mauve and ivory trim—the original wood-work colors, which were discovered under a subsequent layer of paint.

Much of the furniture, such as the white bed with caned head and footboards and the center table are from late 19th-century France. The remaining pieces, including a suite of Cuban mahogany ballroom chairs, were made primarily in England between the late 1700s and early 1900s. In addition to the blue satin covering the sidechair and seat cushions, a striped cotton fabric was used for the draperies, bed furnishings, and upholstery; it was custom matched to the original fabric on the tufted sofa.

RAPHAEL ROOM

The Raphael Room was designed around a series of 18th- and 19th-century engravings after paintings by the Renaissance master Raphael Sanzio (1483–1520). The 14 artworks by several European printmakers depict a range of subjects for which Raphael is famous, including images of the Madonna and the Holy Family and figures from Christianity and classical mythology.

In contrast to the intricate engravings is the room's understated decor. The wallpaper displays a subtle pattern, the English and American furniture boasts little ornamentation beyond its mahogany veneer, and the fabric is a plain cotton velveteen.

The refined appearance of this bedroom reflects both the late-19th-century trend toward less cluttered interiors—a reaction against the excessive opulence of the mid-Victorian era—and the restrained style that arbiters of taste considered appropriate for country retreats.

ABOVE: The blue-and-yellow color scheme of the Raphael Room was popular in the 19th century, with blue especially favored to complement the ruddy tones of mahogany, seen here in the sleigh bed and cupboard secretary.

LEFT: Indicative of the attention paid to every detail during renovation is the variety of textile trims used in the South Tower Room. Four different types of fringe and 40 tassels were chosen to coordinate with the satin and cotton fabrics.

EARLOM ROOM

These elegant guest quarters are part of a suite of four interconnected rooms opened in April 1995 after two years of exhaustive research and restoration. These rooms are located directly above Mr. and Mrs. Vanderbilt's own bedrooms and private sitting room. The suite could have been shared by a family or groups of guests visiting together.

The Earlom Room room was inspired by nine prints in Mr. Vanderbilt's collection by the English engraver Richard Earlom (1745–1822). Archival receipts indicate Mr. Vanderbilt purchased most of these prints from H. Wunderlich and Company, New York.

Central among the eclectic array of furnishings are an armoire and a fall-front bombé bureau—both mid-18th-century examples of Dutch cabinetmakers' command of exacting marquetry decoration. The two-toned wallpaper is an exact reproduction of the original, and the striped cut velvet used for the upholstery, bedspread, and draperies was reproduced from fabric found on the suite of five Spanish Revival chairs placed around the room. The original colors used in the room—olive green paint on the woodwork and ivory paint on the ceiling—were uncovered during the restoration.

NORTH TOWER ROOM

The North Tower Room, one of the largest guest rooms in Biltmore House, is shaped in a graceful oval and decorated in a mixture of styles from the late 18th and early 19th centuries. Furnishings include the 19th-century balloon clock, the delicate armchairs, with their attenuated frame and painted finish, and the languorous chaise lounge, whose lions-paw feet are modeled on a classical motif.

Traces of the original fabric were found in the room and were used in reproducing the printed sateen on the walls and covering several pieces of furniture. Woven in England, the sateen is made of two different designs: an overall floral pattern and a border design. Prints in the room date from the 18th and 19th centuries, and include a mezzotint entitled *The Infant Hercules* by William Ward after Sir Joshua Reynolds.

OPPOSITE: Painted English armchairs surround an elaborately carved tester bed in the North Tower Room. Made in America around 1820, the mahogany bed is dressed in printed cotton sateen to match the wall covering and upholstery— all reproductions of the fabric found in the room before restoration.

ABOVE: This little gilded bulldog, its leash clenched in its mouth, wears a "tag" bearing a photograph of Lila Vanderbilt taken around 1863; it was made by Tiffany and Co. in the mid-19th century.

LEFT: Period designers recommended that bedrooms display colors of "medium scale" and "delicate contrast." The Earlom Room features warm, neutral shades, as seen in the terra-cotta wallpaper and ivory and olive green paint.

Four unique bedrooms were restored and opened to the public in 1999. Located off the Third Floor Living Hall, each guest room was named on original Biltmore House plans after artists or works of art. Each is restored to a different furnishing style, depending on the artist or works of art featured and the clues provided by original wall coverings and other evidence in the rooms.

WATSON ROOM

Named after the 18th-century engraver James Watson (1740–1790), the room reflects the Irish artist's refined neoclassical style. Watson was the favorite engraver of the famous 18th-century portraitist Sir Joshua Reynolds, and George Vanderbilt amassed a large collection of his mezzotints, many of which are on display throughout the room.

The furniture, including a set of mahogany and boxwood twin beds from England, the only twin beds in the Biltmore collection, showcases classical details such as urn shapes and delicate straight legs. A vivid pattern of purple irises and multicolored flowers is featured on

the room's dominant fabric, reproduced from an original late-19th-century textile. This same fabric was found to have been used in a pair of drapery panels and as upholstered seats for the room's two neoclassical side chairs. Both the colors of the fabric and of the room's trim, painted to match the original, coordinate with the fireplace's marble surround. The inkstand on the tambour-top desk is an exquisite combination of early-19th-century Chinese porcelain pieces and late-19th-century French gilt bronze. The glass Tiffany vase with silver webbing on the center of the table dates to 1890.

VAN DYCK ROOM

Anthony Van Dyck (1599–1641) was a prominent 17th-century Dutch painter, and prints of his still-famous portraits adorn this eclectic room, furnished primarily according to a Colonial Revival motif, a style widely used in turn-of-the-century interiors.

The deep green trim and terra-cotta and tan floral wallpaper complement an assortment of 19th-century furniture, including a mahogany chest-on-cabinet in the style of George III, which features painted scenes inspired by Swiss painter Angelica Kauffman (1741–1807), and a decoratively carved walnut bed in the French Empire style. Fabric reproduced from an original in the Biltmore Estate textile collection was used to cover the room's chaise lounge, which is equipped with a silver pull at the rear that allows the piece to recline. The window seat offered guests a place for respite, along with a panoramic view of the Deer Park.

Complementing the room's trim, the fireplace mantel's two shades of original green paint were conserved and stabilized as an example of turn-of-the-century decorative painting technique. Objects from the 1700s, 1800s, and early 1900s decorate the room, including two 18th-century German ceramic figurines.

OPPOSITE: This unusual vase, by the famed art glass maker Louis Comfort Tiffany, demonstrates his mastery of glassmaking techniques. The hand-blown vase features different layers of glass in different colors, with a gold metallic surface and woven sterling silver overlay.

BELOW: This tripod table, made of satinwood, rosewood, mahogany, and maple, is a fine example of the furniture produced by Biltmore Estate Industries at the end of the 19th century. George and Edith Vanderbilt founded Biltmore Estate Industries in 1901 to teach students traditional crafts such as woodworking and weaving.

MORLAND ROOM

Exotic and Rococo Revival influences make the Morland Room, named after popular genre painter George Morland (1736–1804), both unusual and elegant. The focus of the room is the bed canopy, with drapery panels decorated with lively animals, flowers, and hunting scenes. The hand-painted fabric is a careful reproduction of the early-19th-century Indian chintz originally used in this room. Before they arrived at Biltmore, the original fabric panels were hung on the dining room walls of the honeymoon cottage George and Edith Vanderbilt rented in Stressa, Italy.

The oak and linen daybed and arm chair of the Morland Room are covered in coordinating fabric of exotic birds, flowers, and foliage in shades of blue and red. All are highlighted by the light turquoise damask pattern and shimmering silver ground of the room's wallpaper. Scraps of the original wallpaper were found behind light fixtures, then matched to several rolls of the paper still in storage, allowing an exact reproduction to be made.

In addition to the Indian textiles, many decorative objects in the room are in keeping with the 19th-century movement known as exoticism, a fascination with imported items from countries such as India and China. The brilliant jade tree decorating the mantel was made in China in the early 20th century of turquoise, coral, enamel, metal, and other materials. From the same period in China are the glazed ceramic parrot figurines. The porcelain tea caddy is from early-19th-century China, and the ceramic, wood, and brass lamp was created in the early 20th century from a Chinese vase.

BELOW: The canopy fabric was hand-painted by an accomplished artist who spent months reproducing it from the original. The original panels were most likely made for export to Persia, then purchased many decades later by Vanderbilt.

MADONNA ROOM

Prints after masterpieces of the Italian Renaissance, including works by Titian and Raphael, illustrate the theme of the Madonna Room and reflect its Renaissance revival style. A reproduction of the original, the room's wallpaper imitates the look of a 15th-century textile woven with fine gold threads. This shimmering effect is repeated in the gold fabric, roping, and brush fringe used on the room's drapery and upholstery, all of which are identical to the originals.

The room features finely carved Italian-style furniture. At the foot of the bed is a *cassone*, or marriage chest, made in the Italian Renaissance style. To the right of the bed is an Italian chest of drawers made of rosewood, burr maple or birch, and mahogany with intricate gilt wood inlay. A notable decorative object is the

Persian-influenced vase of ceramic, enamel, and metal, which was converted into an electric lamp in the first half of the 20th century.

LEFT: This engraving by the German printmaker Friedrick Muller is after the painting *La Madonna di San Sisto* (the Sistine Madonna), by Renaissance artist Raphael Sanzio. One of his most recognizable works, *La Madonna di San Sisto* features Raphael's famous portrayal of little angels at the bottom of the painting.

*R*estored and opened to the public in 2005, the Fourth Floor originally contained the living quarters for female domestic staff and a centrally located Servants' Hall where servants could relax and socialize. Two additional rooms on this level—distinctly unique—were the Observatory and Architectural Model Room used by George Vanderbilt and his guests.

SERVANTS' BEDROOMS

Whereas the male domestic staff lived on the second floor of the stable and carriage house, most of Biltmore's maids and other female servants lived in 21 assigned rooms on the Fourth Floor. Although their work was hard and their days were long, they were treated fairly. They were paid good wages, were given free room and board, and lived in quarters that had modern amenities such as central heat, indoor plumbing, and electricity.

The servants who lived here had a variety of duties. A housemaid cleaned guest bedrooms, airing out the beds each morning, emptying fireplace ashes, and laying a new fire. A parlor maid cared for public rooms, dusting furniture and art objects, cleaning the floors and rugs, and sometimes waiting table at large formal dinners. Laundresses cleaned, dried, ironed, and folded all the fine bed, bath, and table linens of the household. A visiting lady's maid assisted her mistress with dressing and undressing, preparing her bath and toilet, cleaning, darning, and packing her clothing.

The bedrooms were furnished with wrought iron beds, comfortable rush-seat rocking chairs, and suites of mass-produced oak furniture including wardrobes, chests of drawers, and dressers. Standard bed and bath linens, rugs, lamps, and porcelain pitchers and bowls were also provided.

SERVANTS' BATHROOM

Domestic staff who lived on the Fourth Floor had access to two bathrooms, one at each end of the floor. Each servant also had a chamber pot in her bedroom, helping her avoid a dash down a dark hallway on a cold winter night. There are 43 bathrooms in Biltmore House, an unheard-of number when the house opened in 1895.

RIGHT: Pull-chain toilets had copper-lined oak tanks mounted eight to ten feet above the bowl. These models were more efficient than later flush toilets owing to the use of gravity to flush the bowl rather than the volume of water.

OPPOSITE: According to the 1900 U.S. Census, there were seven housemaids living in bedrooms like this in Biltmore House. Their average age was 32 and they were all single. One was from England, one from Scotland, and five were from North Carolina.

OPPOSITE: While the Servants' Hall was designed for relaxation, its communications technology ensured that servants could be contacted whenever their services were required.

LEFT : The housekeeper, who supervised the house staff, had servants' uniforms laundered off the Estate, as Biltmore's laundries were dedicated to cleaning the family's clothing and household linens.

BELOW: Call boxes were located in Biltmore House to summon staff when necessary. Even when off duty, maids were expected to respond to the ringing of the bell; they would telephone the room where the call originated to see what was needed.

SERVANTS' CLOSET

Biltmore's maids traded their soiled uniforms for freshly laundered ones on a weekly basis. Maids' uniforms typically consisted of a gingham or calico dress during the day, and a more formal black cotton dress in the afternoon and evening, always accompanied by a white starched apron, white collar, cuffs, and cap.

SERVANTS' HALL

Centrally located between two wings of servants' bedrooms, the Servants' Hall offered Biltmore's female staff a place to sit and relax when not on duty. It was simply furnished but comfortable, with oak rocking chairs grouped around a cozy fireplace, a bookcase holding popular titles of the day, and prints on the walls featuring characters from Charles Dickens' novels. Here, maids could socialize, sip a cup of tea, crochet, or read. They were also expected to mend their uniforms as well as any household textiles in their care.

Most maids began their day around 6:00 a.m. and ended work around 9:00 p.m. They were allowed two hours off each afternoon, although they remained on call. Each maid received one afternoon and one evening off per week, as well as a half day every other Sunday.

Some of Biltmore's state-of-the-art technologies can be seen in this room, including the last remaining fire alarm box. The clock on the wall, part of a synchronized clock system, ensured that servants did not have an excuse for being late. Other technological features include a callbox, call buttons, and a telephone that were part of an elaborate communications system that enabled servants to communicate with one another throughout the house.

ARCHITECTURAL MODEL ROOM

In 1889, architect Richard Morris Hunt hired a professional model maker to show his client George Vanderbilt what his grand house would look like. When the model was delivered to Hunt's New York office, it created quite a stir. For some time, the American public had been curious about plans for Mr. Vanderbilt's estate, so it was not surprising that several newspapers chronicled the first public viewing of the model:

The model ... was taken from a wagon in Nassau St. to the office of Richard M. Hunt, the architect ... and a hundred people at once gathered around to speculate about it ... While it was passing, the crowd feasted their eyes on its towers and turrets, its suggestion of magnificent distances and imposing proportions ... It will be a château in the French Renaissance style over 300 feet long, with steep roofs and towers, and sharp gables, and generally elaborate ornamentation. A prominent feature of the château will be a stately octagon tower near the centre. This tower will enclose a massive stone staircase ... The house will be of buff Indiana limestone, will be roofed with dark slate and will, of course, contain the appointments of a luxurious country house ... Mr. Vanderbilt is apparently to have plenty of room for himself and a caller or two should any friend pass his château. (From New York Sun *and* New York Tribune, *October 20, 1889)*

Mr. Vanderbilt chose this room to prominently display the model, which rests on its original base, a large custom-made oak cabinet. On the walls hang architectural prints of French châteaux that inspired the design of Biltmore House.

OBSERVATORY

Strategically positioned at the top of the main entrance tower, the Observatory offers magnificent views of the estate from its central vantage point. This type of room is seemingly unique to America's great mansions of the time.

Mr. Vanderbilt and his guests would climb the elegant spiral staircase in the northwest corner of the room to access the balcony above. This interior balcony, with its decorative wrought iron railing, rings the entire upper level of the Observatory. There, doors lead to an exterior balcony that wraps around the main entrance tower as well as another balcony that encircles the dome of the Grand Staircase. Guests admired the spectacular views of the Esplanade, formal gardens, Conservatory, and the Blue Ridge Mountains in the distance. The balconies also provided close-up views of the roof's dynamic architectural features, including the glass-topped Winter Garden, limestone gargoyles, buttresses, chimneys, and embossed and gilded copper flashing.

On the oak-paneled lower level of the Observatory, a sitting area in front of a wood-burning fireplace provided family and guests with a comfortable place to relax. On a cold day, guests warmed themselves in front of a roaring fire after their time out on the roof.

George Vanderbilt's collaboration with Richard Morris Hunt and Frederick Law Olmsted made possible the creation of Biltmore's architectural and landscape masterpieces. More than any other location in Biltmore House, the Observatory enabled Mr. Vanderbilt to showcase the skills of the architects, landscapers, stone carvers, and numerous other artisans who brought this vision to fruition.

OPPOSITE: The Observatory's lower level features comfortable leather furniture and architectural drawings by Axel Herman Haig (1835–1921).

LEFT AND BELOW: Limestone carvings, statues, and gargoyles, examples of the artistry and talents of stone carvers, adorn the exterior of Biltmore House. Stonecutters were the highest paid of all construction workers at Biltmore, and were members of the Journeymen Stonecutters Association of North America.

The downstairs level of Biltmore House served three distinct purposes. It contained the recreation areas that were used by the Vanderbilts and their guests. It also housed bedrooms and common rooms for the domestic staff. And, as was customary in great country estates, the basement accommodated the pantries and service areas, designed to keep kitchen and laundry clamor far removed from the living quarters upstairs.

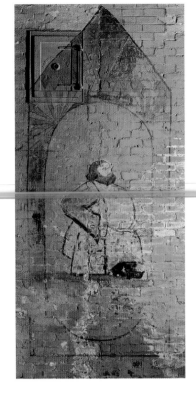

HALLOWEEN ROOM

This one-time storage area was taken over by Cornelia and John Cecil and their guests for a party during the 1920s. Guests personally painted different sections on the walls, thus creating the unusual decoration.

BOWLING ALLEY

The sport of bowling arrived in America in the 1600s with the Dutch settlers and had become a popular pastime by the 1800s, as Victorian men patronized an ever-increasing number of public lanes. At Biltmore both men and women played on one of the first bowling alleys in a private home. The lanes were installed in 1895 by the Brunswick-Balke-Collender Company, a top manufacturer of recreation equipment, and were constructed just as alleys are today. Durable maple planks were laid along the first third of the lanes, which takes the most wear from balls striking the surface, and softer pine decking was used on the remainder, where the balls roll. Balls were returned and pins reset by hand.

DRESSING ROOMS

In the 1890s, each activity had its own dress code, for which ladies and gentlemen had to change their clothes several times a day. To change for recreation, guests used the Dressing Rooms, which were arrayed along separate halls for men and women. These private chambers guaranteed that no one would have to make a long, potentially embarrassing trip from bedroom to basement immodestly attired.

OPPOSITE: The Biltmore House Bowling Alley is one of the earliest examples of an indoor residential bowling alley in the United States.

LEFT: In the main Dressing Room, Cornelia Vanderbilt's ivory grooming set is displayed on a 19th-century English mahogany dressing table; a wooden towel rack holds fresh linens.

ABOVE: This figure is part of the imaginative mural painted for a party in the Halloween Room in the 1920s.

SWIMMING POOL

Biltmore offered a wide range of recreational activities—reflecting not only the need for entertainment in a remote mountain region but also the new emphasis placed on health, fitness, and exercise in the late 1800s. Among the most popular diversions was bathing, which lured Victorians to seashore and lakeside resorts each summer.

The Vanderbilts and their guests, however, could enjoy the water in any season—in a 70,000-gallon indoor pool. Measuring 53 feet long by 27 feet wide by 9½ feet deep, the tilework pool was equipped with such amenities as underwater lighting, safety ropes, and a diving platform. It was fed with hot water through the black hose; the large standing pipe supplied cold water.

Illuminated by chandeliers, the room is also one of the best places to see the fireproof,

terra-cotta tile vaulting that appears in several areas of the House. The vaults were installed according to a technologically advanced building system developed by Rafael Guastavino; his technique was favored by architects because it allowed masonry vaulting to cover wide spans without interior supports during construction.

GYMNASIUM

The Gymnasium was primarily a male precinct. Here, family and guests could tone their muscles with the most up-to-date apparatus, including parallel bars, a chain-driven rowing machine, and wall-mounted pulleys with adjustable weights. The gym also offered barbells, medicine balls, Indian clubs (used to improve hand-eye coordination), and, for the refined athlete, a fencing set. After a vigorous workout, guests could cool down in the showers.

OPPOSITE: Both men and women would have worn bathing costumes that reached down to the knee and up to the neck when enjoying the indoor pool.

BELOW: Much of the 19th-century equipment in the Gymnasium, including the exercise machines, parallel bars, and Indian clubs, was manufactured by A.G. Spalding & Bro., which is still a prominent sporting-goods company today.

PANTRIES

Accommodating the large number of family members, guests, and staff at Biltmore required an extensive larder—especially when provisions were bought in bulk. One bill of sale from 1896, for example, records an order for 28 pounds of lamb legs and loins, 52 pounds of prime beef ribs, 22 broiling and roasting chickens, 62 pounds of muskmelons, and two baskets of peaches.

Groceries from shops in Asheville's Central Market, as well as fresh produce, meats, and dairy products from Biltmore's farm operation, were kept in a series of pantries. The Vegetable Pantry held bins of fruits and vegetables; the Small Pantry stored canned goods; the Housekeeper's Pantry also had canned goods, along with a desk used by the head housekeeper; and the Canning Pantry would have contained produce put up on the Estate.

WALK-IN REFRIGERATORS

Perishables were preserved in two spacious walk-in food coolers that utilized a chilled brine solution circulating through pipes in their interiors. Any sort of refrigeration, let alone cold storage on this scale, was a novelty in the late 1800s, when most homes still relied on iceboxes and springhouses.

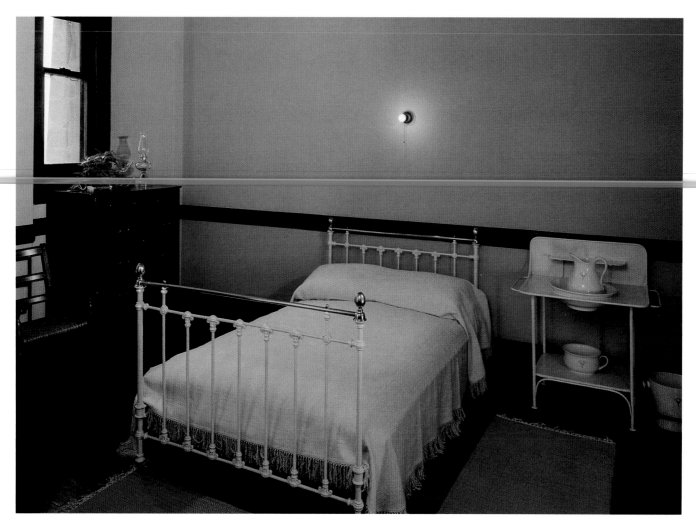

SERVANTS' BEDROOMS

At any one time 30–35 servants might be employed at Biltmore, where they lived in separate halls according to sex and rank. The bedrooms along this corridor represent the private quarters for female members of the kitchen staff, which included cooks' assistants and scullery maids. The rooms are airy and comfortable, with splint-seat chairs, chestnut dressers and wardrobes, and iron beds and washstands holding monogrammed chamber sets.

Based upon their duties and the time of day, service dress changed accordingly. According to oral history compiled from inter-views with estate staff, a cook's assistant wore a red-checked pinafore and a dust cap.

Mounted on the wall outside the bedrooms is one of several call boxes found throughout the House. It is part of an ingenious electric commu-nication system that enabled servants to be summoned with a mere touch of a button from most of the upstairs rooms. The boxes registered a call by ringing a bell and raising a little arrow that indicated the room from which it originated.

OPPOSITE TOP: The spacious Housekeeper's Pantry doubled as a storage area and an office for the head housekeeper.

OPPOSITE BOTTOM: Walk-in coolers stored the quantities of food required for Biltmore's large household.

ABOVE: One of more than 60 staff rooms, this simply furnished Servant's Bedroom includes a cast-iron bed and washstand. First made in the mid 1800s, metal furnishings became popular among health-conscious Victorians, who believed that the metal, unlike wood, did not harbor germs.

OPPOSITE: While bread was sometimes ordered from the French Bakery in Asheville, most baked goods served on Biltmore's tables were made in the Pastry Kitchen.

LEFT: Meats were roasted over an open fire in the rotisserie oven.

BELOW: *The Encyclopaedia of Practical Cookery* was published in London around 1893; it offers instruction on trussing meat and suggestions for "artistic" supper dishes.

PASTRY KITCHEN

Biltmore's kitchen complex, comparable in size to that of a large hotel, was designed for maximum efficiency in food preparation and service. Cooking chores were carried out in three specialized areas, each finished with tiled floors and walls for easy maintenance and each fully stocked with the latest culinary equipment. Staffed by a large number of chefs, cooks, and maids, the kitchens turned out everything from a cup of tea to the lavish dinners that were in vogue at the end of the 19th century.

The Pastry Kitchen was used for fine baking and provided all manner of popular breads and rich confections (a 19th-century cookbook might list hundreds of recipes for cakes and pies). Dough was rolled out on the marble-topped table built in beneath the window; stone slabs like this are preferred by bakers because dough is less likely to stick to the surface. Pastries were baked in two ovens, and dough and perishable ingredients were kept chilled in a refrigerator.

ROTISSERIE KITCHEN

Another cooking area is the Rotisserie Kitchen, which was used for roasting meat, poultry, and game. Such foods—especially pheasant, duck, venison, and other animals brought back from shooting parties—figured heavily on 19th-century menus, often being served for several courses in the same meal.

The iron rotisserie oven, fueled by wood or coal, features a mechanized rotary spit whose speed can be regulated by the electric rheostat mounted on the wall. A drip pan caught grease spatters, and a large overhead vent hood drew off smoke.

MAIN KITCHEN

Most of the cooking at Biltmore took place in the roomy Main Kitchen. Work here started early each morning, when the scullery maid stoked the firebox of the cast-iron cookstove with wood or coal; then the kitchen staff set the work table with knives, choppers, cleavers, braising mallets, and other utensils for the chefs. Conveniently overhead is a battery of polished copper pots and pans—considered the premier cookware for their ability to conduct and retain heat evenly. Displayed around the room are such accessories as a coffee mill and sausage stuffer; in the corner is a large mortar and pestle.

On one side of the stove, which is seven and a half feet long, is a separate grill. On the other side is a tall iron cabinet. Custom made by the New York firm of Duparquet, Huot & Moneuse, it held pots, pans and serving dishes. Of particular note are the cabinet's counter-balanced sliding doors, which, unlike standard hinged doors, allowed access without interfering with the kitchen's work space.

KITCHEN PANTRY

Meals prepared in the basement kitchens had to be transported to the first-floor Butler's Pantry, outside the Banquet Hall, where they were transferred onto serving dishes. (The servants responsible for this chore were familiarly called "tweenies," as they brought food between the kitchens and dining rooms.) While a warming cart was often used for carrying food, meals could also be sent upstairs from the Kitchen Pantry via two dumbwaiters— one manual, one electric; the latter had a lifting capacity of 250 pounds and an operating speed of 100 feet per minute. This room was also used for storing china and washing dishes.

OPPOSITE: The Main Kitchen is well stocked with such tools of the chef's trade as copper cookware, knives, sharpening steels, and choppers. The metal serving trolley, fitted with chafing dishes, was used to transport hot foods to the upstairs dining rooms.

ABOVE: The electric dumbwaiter in the Kitchen Pantry has push-button controls and runs 38 feet between the Basement and Second Floor.

BELOW: This hand-cranked, tin meat "hasher" was the 19th-century equivalent of a food processor.

SERVANTS' DINING ROOM

With the exception of professional chefs, who dined in the Main Kitchen, all of Biltmore's domestic staff took their meals in the Servants' Dining Room. The head chef's assistant, or "second chef," prepared food for the servants, while a dining-hall maid served all their meals. She was also responsible for keeping the room clean and maintaining all the servants' dishes and cutlery.

Servants normally received breakfast, dinner, supper, mid-morning and mid-afternoon snacks daily, with dinner (served at 12:00 noon) being the heartiest meal of the day. It typically consisted of a soup course, a meat course with accompanying vegetables, and a dessert course. Supper for the staff was served early, around 5:00 or 5:30 p.m., so that servants were available to prepare and serve the Vanderbilts' meals later in the evening.

ORGAN MOTOR ROOM

This room was designed to house the blower mechanism for the Banquet Hall organ and contains the air chase and electrical wiring necessary to power the 19th-century Skinner instrument. Because an organ was not installed when the House was built, the room was used for storage until 1998, when an organ was finally installed.

WORK ROOM

This room is used by the floral design staff to prepare the cut-flower arrangements seen throughout the House. Plants from the gardens and greenhouses have always played an important role in the decor at Biltmore.

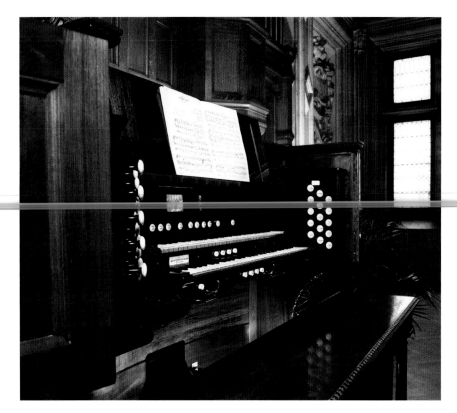

OPPOSITE: Staff ate in the Servants' Dining Room around a mahogany dining table, seated on bentwood chairs.

ABOVE: This 1916 pipe organ made by the Ernest M. Skinner Company, is powered by the blower mechanism in the Basement Organ Motor Room. The organ was restored and installed in the Banquet Hall in 1998. It features two keyboards, a pedalboard, a roll player, 47 speaking pipes in the front row, and 30 dumb pipes in the back row.

LEFT: An elaborate system of ducts carry compressed air from the Organ Motor Room through original 100-year-old air shafts to the Organ Loft in the Banquet Hall.

BROWN LAUNDRY

Like the kitchens, Biltmore's laundry complex was a convenient, efficient operation organized on a commercial scale. In four specialized work rooms, the laundresses and maids handled the substantial quantities of clothing and linens generated by family, guests, and servants.

The Brown Laundry was used for hand washables and is equipped with deep tubs in which dirt was laboriously scrubbed away on fluted-tin washboards. The wooden "cradle" is a hand-agitated mechanical washing machine from the early 1900s. On the table are various pressing devices, including fluting irons with ridged rollers for crimping pleats and ruffles and double-pointed sadirons that were heated on a special laundry stove. Next door is the Laundresses' Toilet, which was for staff use.

MAIN LAUNDRY

The equipment in the Main Laundry is similar to the state-of-the-art machinery originally installed in 1895. In addition to a belt-driven barrel washer are an extractor, which was used to spin out excess water, and a mangle, which was used for pressing.

DRYING ROOM

On the right side of the Main Laundry is the Drying Room; all laundry was dried indoors, so that the laundress would never be at the mercy of the weather. After the laundry was wrung as dry as possible, it was draped over an innovative system of rolling wooden racks that could be pulled out from a wall cabinet for air drying or pushed back into niches that were heated with electric coils running along the floor.

OPPOSITE: Linens aired on pull-out racks, which slid into recesses in a wall cabinet where heat from floor-mounted electric coils speeded drying.

ABOVE: In the Brown Laundry, hand washing was done with wooden washboards in the enameled basins.

BELOW: This sadiron, made by the Enterprise Manufacturing Company of Philadelphia, features a detachable stay-cool wooden handle that could be used interchangeably on iron bodies heating on a laundry stove.

Set off from the rest of the First Floor is the Bachelors' Wing, a private, masculine section of the House with its own entrance through a covered carriage porch off the stable courtyard. It was connected to the single men's upstairs guest rooms by a separate stairwell and boasted specialized game and sitting areas where gentlemen could discuss business and politics, relax with a pipe, or relive exploits from a day's shooting party.

SMOKING ROOM

Smoking, like gambling and hunting, was primarily a male prerogative in the 1800s, and the smoking parlor became a required feature in fashionable country houses soon after it appeared in mid century. Here, men savored the pleasure of a cigar or pipe, perhaps as an accompaniment to a glass of after-dinner spirits; they might even try the new machine-rolled cigarettes being produced in the tobacco centers of North Carolina. Guests could also select a leather-bound book from the collection and read before the fire in the plush 17th-century-style sofas and chairs.

GUN ROOM

Guests at Biltmore never wanted for outdoor recreation. There was horseback riding, carriage driving, fishing, hiking, and, of course, hunting—

the quintessential country house amusement. To ensure a good day's shooting, Mr. Vanderbilt had the Estate stocked with a plentiful supply of deer, quail, pheasant, and other wild game.

The Gun Room pays tribute to the popularity of the sport, which had developed into such a passion by the 1870s that the proper house was considered incomplete without this special shrine. As was customary, the room is outfitted with glass-front cases for firearms (no longer in the collection) stored in custom-built racks, and for an array of animal trophies. On the walls are 19th-century prints with sporting themes after the British artists Sir Joshua Reynolds (1723–92) and James Ward (1769–1859), and on the tables are bronze sculptures of game animals.

RIGHT: In turn-of-the-century society, smoking was an acceptable practice— for men at least—as long as it was done in a separate room. The Smoking Room provided a comfortable retreat for male guests to enjoy after-dinner cigars.

OPPOSITE: With its ebonized woodwork and gold-leaf wall covering, the Gun Room is a handsome showcase for hunting trophies, such as this game bird (above), and sporting art. The room also displayed guns; collecting antique and contemporary firearms was a popular gentlemen's pastime.

In the preautomotive age of the late 19th century, horses and horse-drawn vehicles played an important role in both transportation and recreation. Reflecting their significance is the 12,000-square-foot stable complex at the north end of the front facade—a facility that was as carefully designed and completely equipped as the House itself.

STABLE

Like his father, who was so devoted to his trotters that he built an indoor riding ring for them, Mr. Vanderbilt took exceptional care of his horses. As many as 25 riding and driving horses, along with 20 carriages, were sheltered at Biltmore in a modern stable complete with electricity, plumbing, glazed-brick walls, and brass fixtures and hardware.

The Stable also contained all the attendant service areas, including rooms for saddles, tack, harness, blankets, and feed, as well as living quarters for single male servants. Among the staff of stable hands were grooms, a harness man, an exerciser, and a coachman, whose job entailed supervising the grooming of the horses, driving family and guests in the carriages, and assisting riders with their mounts.

Today, the Stable has been converted into an avenue of shops offering books, confections, toys, Christmas ornaments, and decorative accessories. The largest shop is located in the former Carriage House, while the Stable Café now occupies the old horse stable—with tables tucked into the original box stalls. In the courtyard, where horses' hooves and carriage wheels once clattered on the brick pavers, tables and chairs are set out for dining or relaxing in the historic setting.

BILTMORE™
Gardens & Trails

From mountain forest to manicured flower bed to valley farm, the grounds at Biltmore were unparalleled in scale and diversity when conceived in the 1880s. They remain one of the premier achievements of American's foremost landscape architect, Frederick Law Olmsted. His genius for design and his love of nature are visible today throughout the 8,000-acre Estate, where his plan and many of the original plantings have been preserved.

W̲hat is now a lush, mature landscape was once a depleted tract of worn-out farms and cutover woodlands. Olmsted transformed the site into a 250-acre park, designed in the English pastoral mode to complement the architecture of the House, take advantage of the native flora and terrain, and provide varied settings for outdoor recreation. Beginning with the formal lawns around the House, the grounds become increasingly naturalistic as they spread out toward a managed woodland that looks so wild it appears never to have been touched. The Estate includes miles of scenic carriage drives, several lakes and ponds, and thousands of acres of managed forests.

APPROACH ROAD

An integral part of Biltmore's landscape is the three-mile-long Approach Road. It begins at the Lodge Gate, the pebbledash gatehouse at the edge of Biltmore Village, and ends at the sphinx-topped stone pillars near the Front Lawn. In between it traverses a "garden" as meticulously planned as the formal flower beds.

Olmsted designed the Approach Road to heighten anticipation of seeing the House by having visitors first wind slowly through a woodland. The idea, he said, was to evoke a sense of mystery while creating the "... sensation of passing through the remote depths of a natural forest." And so the drive snakes along the ravines through dense border plantings of rhododendron, mountain laurel, and azalea, passing from woods to open meadow and back again to groves of hemlock and pine—with no distant views to interrupt the intimate effect. At every turn is a new surprise: a stream, a pool, a blanket of wildflowers, a thicket of river cane.

In developing this "natural" landscape, Olmsted started virtually from scratch, sculpting the land before installing any plant material. Many of the trees and shrubs he used were transplants collected as seedlings from the Carolina plains, piedmont, and mountains. These native specimens were supplemented with plants grown in Biltmore's own nursery, which had been estab-lished in 1889 with stock and seeds from the acclaimed Arnold Arboretum near Boston, as well as from other nurseries in America and Europe.

Because the family traveled frequently —"Mr. Vanderbilt and his guests always miss the best of the bloom," lamented Olmsted— the Approach Road was planted with a variety of deciduous trees, conifers, and flowering shrubs that would provide interest year-round. There were even exotic species, such as bamboo, to add a subtropical character to the landscape. The design was acknowledged to be a success, even by so particular a critic as Richard Morris Hunt. "Hasn't Olmsted done wonders with the approach road?" he wrote in an 1892 letter to Mr. Vanderbilt. "It alone will give him lasting fame."

OPPOSITE: Designed by Hunt, the Lodge Gate was built with bricks and roof tiles made on the Estate; it is faced with a rough stucco finish called pebbledash.

ABOVE: Mr. Vanderbilt, standing beside Olmsted (far right, front row), poses with the crew during construction of the Approach Road in 1892.

LEFT: The drive is lined with dense border plantings to create a mysterious, intimate effect.

GARDENS AND TRAILS | 93

ABOVE: Young Cornelia takes a dip in the Front Lawn fountain in this circa 1910 photo.

BELOW LEFT: Olmsted's original plan for the Home Grounds covered the design for garden areas around the House—from the Esplanade to the Walled Garden.

BELOW RIGHT: The Rampe Douce was already completed by December 1892, while the rest of the Esplanade and the House were still under construction.

OPPOSITE: The statue of Diana stands before a double grove of hemlock trees that seem to form the letter "V"; the Rampe Douce is at the base of the slope. The lawn between was originally mowed by a horse- or mule-drawn mowing machine.

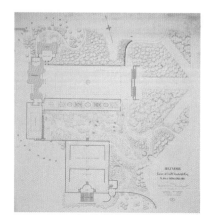

ESPLANADE

At the end of the Approach Road, Biltmore House at last comes into view, rising before a trim, level lawn lined with double rows of tulip trees. The contrast in style between the naturalistic drive and the formal grounds immediately surrounding the House is deliberate: Olmsted used this area to form a transition between the stately building and the wilder, outlying landscape.

The entire forecourt is called the Esplanade and was inspired by the gardens at the mid-17th-century Château de Vaux-le-Vicomte near Melun, France. It incorporates the Front Lawn, with its softly splashing fountain, and the majestic Rampe Douce (meaning "gentle incline"), a graduated stairway zigzagging along a rough-cut limestone wall. Beyond stretches a grassy slope known as the Vista, with a statue of Diana, goddess of the hunt, marking the summit—the perfect vantage point for viewing the House against its backdrop of mountains.

TERRACES

Visitors at Biltmore, who would often stay for weeks or months at a time, were encouraged to use the entire landscape—whether by hiking through the forest, playing lawn games, or simply watching the sunset from the comfort of a garden bench. The Terraces were designed for those who preferred to stay close by the House. Guests could enjoy the shade of the Library Terrace, which is sheltered by an arbor of fragrant wisteria and colorful trumpet creeper. Or they might stroll to the South Terrace, once the site of a bowling green, to relax in the limestone Tea House and take in the spectacular panorama of the Deer Park, Lagoon, and Blue Ridge Mountains; Mount Pisgah, at 5,721 feet, is the highest peak in the distance.

ITALIAN GARDEN

Three symmetrical pools mark the Italian Garden, where gravel paths and manicured lawns form an ordered composition. Enclosed by a hemlock hedge and stone walls, the garden was intended as a separate outdoor "room" and is decorated with classical statuary, jardinieres, and benches. While the space was meant for quiet contemplation, it was also used for recreation: tennis and croquet were played on the grassy area nearest the House. After their game, guests could slip into the basement to change clothes through the door under the stairway.

PERGOLA

Another broad stone stair leads to the wisteria and trumpet creeper-covered Pergola overlooking the former lawn tennis court. The shady bower provided a cool spot for spectators, who could also enjoy the soft music of trickling wall fountains.

SHRUB GARDEN

In contrast to the formal Italian Garden is the four-acre Shrub Garden, or Ramble—a rich, picturesque landscape with hundreds of woody plants. Olmsted chose this protected site for a "secluded and genial" garden where guests could "ramble" along meandering paths through an ever-changing pageant of plants. Filled with specimens that provide a succession of color— from the winter jasmine that opens in February to the cutleaf Japanese maples that blush red until frost—this area features such old-fashioned shrubs as lilac, viburnum, forsythia, and honeysuckle. Reflecting the era's interest in plants from the Far East, the garden also features numerous species native to Asia, including Japanese stewartia, Kousa dogwood, and, added after the turn of the century, Yoshino cherry.

OPPOSITE: Water lilies and Egyptian lotus fill the pools in the Italian Garden; in warm weather the bed in the central pool is stocked with cannas and ornamental grasses, both popular in turn-of-the-century gardens.

BELOW: A path threads past spring-flowering cherry, forsythia, and spirea in the Ramble. With the blooms of azaleas, dogwoods, and wisteria soon to follow, the garden is so lush and varied that the promenade seems longer than it actually is.

WALLED GARDEN

The gate at the lower edge of the Ramble opens into the four-acre Walled Garden, which Olmsted had planned with mixed plots of flowers, fruits, and vegetables typical of an English kitchen garden. Mr. Vanderbilt, however, insisted on "a garden of ornament rather than utility," reasoning that the Estate farm would supply produce instead.

Two arbors totalling 236 feet entwined with some original grapevines form the spine of the symmetrical plan, which comprises flower beds arranged in patterns similar to an Elizabethan knot garden. The garden blooms with a progression of color, starting in spring with daffodils, hyacinths, and tulips. These are followed in summer by some 40 varieties of annuals, including dahlias, zinnias, and globe amaranth, while fall brings a multi-hued display of chrysanthemums. Along the outer walls are espaliered fruit trees, rose-of-Sharon, and pyracantha—which require trimming at least six times per growing season—as well as perennial borders of bleeding heart, peony, iris, and daylily.

ROSE GARDEN

The lower half of the walled area is planted with 2,300 roses in 250 varieties, including more than 100 All-America Rose Selections. While most of the plants are modern varieties, the garden also boasts a number of heirloom roses, especially varieties grown in Vanderbilt's time such as Paul Neyron (introduced in 1869) and American Beauty (introduced in 1875).

CONSERVATORY

The glass-roofed conservatory was designed by Hunt, rebuilt in 1957, and restored in 1999. It provides flowers and plants for Biltmore House and tender bedding plants for the gardens just as it did in the Vanderbilts' day. The building, sheltered in a valley for protection, was constructed at the lower end of the garden so as to not obstruct views from the House. Its central room is a "Palm House," where a large collection of palms, ferns, and other foliage plants thrive. Annexes include a cool house, hot house, and orchid house. The lower level has been converted into A Gardener's Place shop, offering plants and garden accessories.

OPPOSITE: The Walled Garden is abloom with thousands of daffodils and Dutch tulips in spring. Such enclosed gardens were common in England and northern Europe because they trapped sunshine and shielded plants from wind, creating a hospitable microclimate.

ABOVE: Among the 250 varieties in the Rose Garden is the Pink Peace rose, a fragrant, long-blooming hybrid tea introduced in 1959.

BELOW: The beds in front of the Conservatory are filled with buddleia, asters, sunflowers, and other colorful plants that attract butterflies.

SPRING GARDEN

Sheltered by a cathedral grove of white pines and hemlocks, the Spring Garden lies in a secluded pocket just beyond the Ramble. The garden may have been named for the two small springs found here, which Olmsted diverted underground to create a stream flowing into the Azalea Garden. He also called it the Vernal Garden for its spring-blooming shrubs, such as forsythia, spirea, deutzia, and mock orange.

AZALEA GARDEN

A wood-chip path connects the Spring Garden to the 20-acre Azalea Garden, the largest and "lowest" of the gardens that occupy a series of hollows below the House. Olmsted called it the Glen, for its protected valley site. Today, however, it is named—and renowned—for its superb array of azaleas.

These plants were assembled by Chauncey Beadle, a Cornell-educated horticulturist who was hired "temporarily" in 1890 to oversee the nursery but stayed on until his death in 1950, eventually becoming estate superintendent. Over the course of 15 years, Beadle and three friends, who called themselves the "Azalea Hunters," traveled from New England to Florida to Texas studying and gathering native specimens. In 1940, he donated his entire collection of 3,000 plants—one of the largest collections in the world—to Biltmore Estate.

More than 1,000 azaleas, representing 14 native species and countless hybrids, now thrive in the garden, growing alongside metasequoias, magnolias, dogwoods, and a number of conifers that Beadle added from an arboretum that was never completed. Included in the vast variety of plants are such rarities as the Florida torreya, now facing extinction in its natural habitat, and the Franklinia, which disappeared from the wild in 1790.

DEER PARK

Covering 250 acres to the south and west of Biltmore House is a wooded area known as a deer park, inspiring the name of an Estate restaurant. Scenic game preserves like this were often used for hunting on English country estates. The natural design, composed of rolling meadows and groves of poplar, beech, oak, and hickory, was inspired by the "pastoral" landscape style developed in the 1700s.

BASS POND AND LAGOON

Water features were an important aspect of the pastoral landscape, and Olmsted planned two for the Estate. The Bass Pond, created from an old creek-fed millpond, is just south of the Azalea Garden. Guests out for a walk at the "end" of the gardens could rest at the boathouse or take in the view from a footbridge spanning a waterfall that spills into a rocky ravine. In addition to its beauty, the Pond is remarkable for an engineering feat: Olmsted installed a flume system for flood control that pipes debris-filled storm water under the lake bed.

The placid Lagoon is located on Old River Road and acts as a mirror for the maple, sweet gum, and river birch lining its shore and for the western facade of the House. Like the Bass Pond, the Lagoon was used for recreation.

OPPOSITE: The tranquil Lagoon was used by guests for fishing and rowing.

ABOVE: The rustic boathouse overlooking the Bass Pond offers a peaceful resting place after a garden stroll; Olmsted incorporated similar structures into his designs for many public parks.

BELOW: In autumn the hardwoods in the Deer Park put on a splendid foliage display. Olmsted created such serene pastoral settings to have a soothing effect on the spirit.

WALKING TRAILS

Near the Bass Pond and Azalea Garden are four walking trails carrying out Frederick Law Olmsted's philosophy that Biltmore's landscape should be enjoyed to its fullest. The trails are based on Olmsted's early plans for the Bass Pond, providing vantage points to observe birds and animals that live on the Estate.

The Bass Pond Trail offers a spectacular view of the brick bridge across the pond. The Meadow Trail loops through the Deer Park, with views of the pond and wildflower meadows.

Passing through a shady grove, the Creekside Trail showcases a bald cypress more than 100 feet high growing on the opposite bank. Part of the Woodland Trail follows an old farm road dating to the 1880s; today, the area is evidence of the Estate's reforestation efforts. A rustic bridge some 50 feet long of native black locust, oak, and pine spans a spring-fed brook in the wooded hollow.

FOREST

While the rich woodlands blanketing much of the Estate seem to be virgin stands, many were planted as part of a comprehensive land management program initiated by Olmsted and developed by Gifford Pinchot, the first American-born trained forester to practice in the United States.

Biltmore's woods had been badly over-farmed, overcut, and burned before Mr. Vanderbilt acquired the property—so much that Olmsted advised him against installing an extensive European-style park. The designer proposed turning the site into productive timberland that would contribute to the Estate and also represent America's first organized attempt at forestry. In 1891, Olmsted enlisted Pinchot to rehabilitate the woodland. Pinchot's plan—identifying varieties, selectively thinning, and planting for maximum timber yield—served as a national model.

Pinchot left Biltmore in 1895 to establish what would become the U.S. Forest Service; continuing his work was Dr. Carl Schenck (1868–1955), a prominent German forester Mr. Vanderbilt invited to America. Besides installing experimental plantations of indigenous species, Schenck founded the Biltmore Forest School in 1898. The school operated until 1913, teaching conservation techniques still influential today.

There are now about 4,500 acres of forest at Biltmore, with timber sales providing some financial support for Estate operations. The land is actively managed to improve the quality of soil, water, and wildlife habitats, and to preserve the forest in harmony with Olmsted's historic landscape.

OPPOSITE: The shade-dappled Woodland Trail crosses a 50-foot bridge crafted of black locust rails and posts, pine beams, and oak planking.

BELOW: Forester Gifford Pinchot (left) was photographed on the Estate with Mr. Vanderbilt (second from right) and guests around 1895; Pinchot went on to found the Yale University School of Forestry and the U.S. Forest Service.

BILTMORE™
Winery

Opened in 1985, Biltmore Winery is a fitting addition to Mr. Vanderbilt's vision. The enterprise recalls the historic estate wineries of Europe and also reaffirms the century-old Biltmore tradition of self-sufficiency. Although one of the "youngest" wineries in America, it is the most visited and among the most acclaimed, having earned more than 700 awards since its inception.

Just as Biltmore House preserves the architectural heritage of the Estate, the Winery perpetuates its agricultural legacy. Rich farmland that once supported produce crops has been given over to vineyards, and the former dairy complex now houses the extensive wine-making operation. The Winery also carries on Mr. Vanderbilt's interest in technology and insistence on quality: state-of-the-art equipment is used at every step in producing Biltmore's premier wines.

WINERY

The Winery is located in a building designed by Richard Howland Hunt and farm manager George Weston for Biltmore's Dairy, which began in 1896 as part of a large farm operation that also included produce and livestock. Like Biltmore House, the Dairy Barn was thoroughly modern, from the ice-cooled pipeline that delivered milk into a creamery across the street to the underground rail system that hauled away used stall bedding. The Dairy was a tremendous success: its eggs, milk, butter, and cheese were sold throughout Asheville and the Southeast, and ice cream was served at a dairy bar next to this main building.

The facility was occupied by the Dairy until 1957 and was reopened as the Winery in 1985 after a three-year renovation. Covering 96,500 square feet, the handsome pebbledash building proved remarkably adaptable in being converted to a new use. The old haymow became visitors' areas, and the three wings of the barn, where more than 200 cows had been housed, were turned into tasting and bottling rooms. The structural vaults in the basement, which have a constant temperature of 54 degrees—the perfect temperature for a wine cellar—were an ideal place to keep wines and sparkling wines during aging.

OPPOSITE: After a three-year renovation, the former Dairy became the Winery. Its central clock tower originally had only three working clock faces; a fourth face was added in the 1985 renovation.

ABOVE: Biltmore Dairy Farms milkmen, seen here around 1930, delivered milk, cheese, butter, and eggs in their fleet of dry-ice-cooled trucks.

LEFT: An aerial photograph from the 1920s shows the unusual design of the Dairy Barn, with its three long wings. Today these have been converted to house the Winery's Tasting and Bottling Rooms.

ABOVE: At harvest time, clusters of grapes are picked by hand under the direction of Biltmore's French wine master.

OPPOSITE: Covering about 94 acres along the banks of a lake, which was created to aid plant growth, the vineyards produce more than 250 tons of grapes each year.

VINEYARDS

Biltmore began experimenting with wine making in the 1970s. The first vines were planted in 1971, in a plot near the Conservatory greenhouses, and the first wines produced six years later (it generally takes five years for vines to mature enough to yield a full crop). The regional climate—with its warm days, cool nights, and mild winter temperatures—is quite hospitable to grapes; in fact, wine has been made in North Carolina as far back as the colonial era.

While the vineyards were initially planted with indigenous grapes, then with French-American hybrids, they have now been given over to *Vitis vinifera*—the European grape species from which all world-class wines are produced. Some 56,000 vines thrive on more than 94 gently sloping acres in the western portion of the Estate, constituting one of the largest plantings of vinifera grapes east of the Mississippi River. A lake was constructed on the site to insure a favorable microclimate: the water creates a little pocket of warmth beside the vineyards, helping combat the late spring frosts that threaten young buds.

Among the grape varietals under cultivation are Cabernet Sauvignon, Cabernet Franc, and Merlot, which yield red wines, along with Chardonnay, Riesling, and Viognier, which are used in making white wines. Chardonnay grapes also go into the sparkling wines.

Each year between late August and mid October, Biltmore's employees gather in the vineyards to pick grapes under the supervision of Bernard Delille, a classically trained wine master from France. The clusters are painstakingly picked by hand to ensure that only ripe, perfect "berries" are selected. With a harvest exceeding 250 tons of grapes annually, the vineyards satisfy a fourth of the Winery's production capacity.

WINE PRODUCTION

Wine making at Biltmore is a combination of state-of-the-art technology and Old World technique. Although the Winery is one of the leading researchers in viticulture in the eastern United States and uses the most advanced equipment, it follows centuries-old practices developed in Europe to produce the finest wines. As a result, its wines have earned a remarkable number of awards—including gold and double-gold medals in prestigious national and international competitions.

The Winery produces 160,000 cases of wine each year in more than 20 varieties. The production process begins in the Fermentation Room, where the "must," or crushed grapes, is piped into a series of stainless-steel fermentation tanks, each holding between 3,000 and 5,000 gallons. Grapes for red wine are processed with their skins for flavor and color in computer-controlled rotating tanks for 8 to 21 days, whereas grapes for white wine are fermented without their skins in vertical tanks for up to a month. During fermentation the sugar in the grapes converts to alcohol; when all the sugar is "fermented out," the wine is dry.

The next step is aging, which develops the wine's flavor and bouquet. Because the grapes differ from year to year depending on weather and rainfall, the wine master must determine the proper treatment and aging time for each vintage. Generally, the white wines are aged briefly in the stainless-steel tanks and the red wines are aged for one to two years in oak casks located in the Barrel Room.

The aged wines are bottled in an atmosphere-controlled "clean" room, where the air is filtered and exchanged about every 60 seconds—indicative of the Winery's high standards for purity. Running along an automated assembly line, sterilized bottles are filled, corked, capped, and labeled at a rate of 65 per minute.

Sparkling wines are bottled by hand, a process that visitors can view several times each year. These wines are made by the *méthode champenoise*—the method used for French champagne—which calls for a second fermentation in the bottle to produce the distinctive sparkle. At the end of that two-year process, the bottles are stored neck down on special racks and turned daily. This technique, known as riddling, traps sediment, which is then frozen and disgorged; to replace this "lost" liquid, the bottles are topped with a *dosage*, a special mixture of wine and sugar, before being corked. Riddling racks are on display in the Cellars, where wines and wine barrels are stored in the stone alcoves.

OPPOSITE: Two white wines—Chardonnay and Sauvignon Blanc—and all the red wines age in casks made of French or American oak; tannin and other natural substances in the wood, which is lightly charred, enhance the wine's flavor.

ABOVE: Biltmore Estate Cabernet Sauvignon has won gold medals in prestigious wine competitions; overall, the Estate's wines have earned more than 700 regional, national, and international awards.

LEFT: Sparkling wines, which must ferment in the bottle for two years in a cool, dark place, are stored in the Cellars. After fermentation is complete, the bottles are placed at an inverted angle on a riddling rack.

TASTING ROOM

The spacious Tasting Room, with giant scissor trusses crisscrossing beneath the clerestory ceiling, was originally home to 80 cows. Now renovated into a welcoming setting, guests are invited to sample different wines at their own pace; for novices and connoisseurs alike, part of the pleasure of wine is discovering new varieties that suit their individual palates. Specially trained hosts are always on hand to assist with tasting techniques, discuss the characteristics of different varietals (a "varietal" wine is named for the dominant grape variety from which it is made), and explain how wine can be used to complement food.

The broad range of Biltmore Estate wines—from the light, delicate Chardonnay Sur Lies to the full-bodied Cardinal's Crest—offers numerous possibilities for enhancing a meal. A classic dry white varietal, such as Sauvignon Blanc, for example, is considered particularly good with seafood. A semisweet Chardonnay might be recommended to accompany pasta or poultry. Dry red wines, such as Cabernet Sauvignon, bring out the flavor of meat dishes. Sweet rosés make delicious dessert wines—especially with fruits or chocolate—while sparkling wine can be served with all types of food and with any course.

Adjacent to the Tasting Room—on the site of the former ice cream bar—is a large shop featuring a complete selection of Biltmore Estate wines, wine glasses and other accessories, gourmet foods, and cookbooks. The Wine Shop also includes a Wine Bar and demonstration kitchen where guests can learn more about pairing food with wine.

ABOVE: The Cecil family crest adorns the Tasting Room at the Winery.

RIGHT: Known for their record-breaking milk production, Biltmore's pedigreed Jersey cows are shown here around 1939 awaiting their turn in the milking parlor. The barn features a clerestory ceiling, which admits natural light, and scissor trusses, a type of flexible roof support that gives with changes in humidity.

OPPOSITE: Bright open spaces and awards create a festive atmosphere in the Tasting Room, where guests can sample Biltmore wines.

BILTMORE™
River Bend Farm

Opened in 2004, River Bend Farm and its unique historic horse barn complex, farmyard, and kitchen garden, connect guests with another side of Biltmore: one that explores its agricultural legacy and Mr. Vanderbilt's vision of a self-supporting estate. The farm is a popular destination for guests of all ages, offering insights into families who lived and worked on the Estate and the role it has played in Biltmore life for more than a century.

Agriculture has been the heart of Biltmore since before George Vanderbilt's arrival. Today, River Bend Farm tells the stories of the families who lived and worked on the Estate's dairy and farming operations, and made Biltmore a model for innovative agricultural practices. Through the renovated 1902 horse barn, farmyard, and kitchen garden, guests get a sense of the effort required for such a large agricultural endeavor.

RIVER BEND BARN

Originally referred to as "Barns and Horse Stable" on a 1900 architectural drawing by Richard Howland Hunt, this unique complex was located at the center of the Estate's dairy and farming operations that included poultry, sheep and hog farms, and a truck farm or market garden for vegetables. The name River Bend Farm was historically applied to one of the many smaller farms Mr. Vanderbilt purchased in the same vicinity of the "River Bend Peninsula" of the French Broad River.

The barn complex consisted of two buildings with four attached sheds forming an octagon enclosing a central yard. The sheds were open, allowing for easy access to equipment stored out of the weather. Original plans indicate the central stable wing had 14 box stalls for draft horses and mules, and two "loose box stalls" for foaling, arranged in two rows along a central corridor.

On the opposite end, a stairway led to the second floor where animal feed was stored; large ramps on the east and west ends of the barn also accessed this floor. Loads of corn and hay were delivered via the ramps; corn was deposited into corncribs and hay was lifted to the third floor hayloft. A system of grain bins and chutes stored and moved grains like oats and cracked corn for feeding animals on the lower level.

The ground level of the barn was open on two sides for easy movement of wagons and other equipment. Over time, a number of changes altered the original appearance, with the most significant change being a 1950s addition that ran along the length of the barn's north side.

Rooms on the south side of the complex were identified on the 1900 architectural drawing as a repair shop, laborers' room, smithy, small tools room, and four separate "stores" or storage rooms.

From the 1890s well into the 1950s, the barn was alive with activity from well before dawn until well after dusk. All services required to maintain the farm animals and equipment, including the blacksmith and repair shops, were located here, as well as stables for draft horses and mules.

Soon after World War II, modern tractors, trucks, and other mechanical equipment replaced horses and mules for transportation and agrarian use. Portions of the complex then served as a vehicle repair shop, carpenter's shop, company store, and equipment storage area.

OPPOSITE: The historic 1902 barn was restored more than a century later.

BELOW: Central to the River Bend Farm complex is a barn that housed the Estate's workhorses, blacksmith's shop, wagon repair shop, laborer's room, storage shed, and feed for farm animals.

BELOW: Carrying on the Estate legacy of agricultural life, contemporary craftspeople like blacksmiths demonstrate their skills at River Bend Barn.

BOTTOM: Twelve homes for estate managers and workers, part of The Line, are seen in this archival photo of the farm.

OPPOSITE: Agricultural workers and estate residents at the Market Garden, photographed in front of an elaborate display of estate-raised produce.

FARM LIFE

Next to River Bend Barn were two manager's cottages, two smaller houses, and a row of eight workers' houses to the west known as The Line. Also nearby was Antler Hall, a large pre-existing boarding house divided into apartments for the families of Biltmore Dairy workers.

The workers and families who lived in this area formed a closely-knit community that became known as the farm and dairy village. Many families called this area home through the years, with their lives revolving around the village and horse barn. Children met to ride the "school bus," a farm wagon fitted with cross seats and drawn by two farm horses, to school in Biltmore Village outside the Estate's entrance. Estate employees and their families purchased many household supplies they could not produce at home or in their gardens at the farm store, first located in the horse barn and later in the main dairy.

Tenant farmers and their families who lived on the Estate's west side used two ferries to cross the French Broad River to pick up supplies or attend social events like the much anticipated Estate Exhibition that Edith Vanderbilt sponsored for employees and their families. She was a frequent visitor to the dairy village, establishing sewing and cooking classes for the women and girls, a Sunday school, and night school classes for adults.

Today, guests can step back into the everyday lives of families who raised livestock, tended crops, and worked at Biltmore Dairy in the late 19th and early 20th centuries. River Bend Barn is alive again with blacksmiths, woodworkers, old-fashioned music, storytelling, and farm life demonstrations. Interpretive exhibits of agricultural equipment evoke memories of the rural past. The Mercantile offers handcrafted wares from the resident blacksmiths and woodworkers, while the Creamery tempts with ice cream treats, sandwiches, and other favorites.

ABOVE: More than 100 varieties of vegetables, fruits, herbs, and flowers thrive in the five-acre Kitchen Garden.

KITCHEN GARDEN

Established in 1994, the Kitchen Garden has developed into a large-scale production garden for Biltmore's unique "Field to Table" program as well as a showcase for gardening demonstrations.

When George Vanderbilt established Biltmore, he hired Frederick Law Olmsted to plan and lay out beautifully landscaped gardens and grounds around his grand château. Olmsted suggested that it would be a great investment of Mr. Vanderbilt's time and capital to create a working estate as well, with productive forests and fields that would become a source of pride and a model for the country. Mr. Vanderbilt agreed, and hired agricultural experts to plan and develop his farm operations that included a Truck Farm or Market Garden, which supplied many varieties of vegetables and fruits for the Vanderbilts and their guests.

The Kitchen Garden, with more than five acres of vegetables, fruits, and herbs in production, takes inspiration from this legacy. The Kitchen Garden supplies estate chefs with a wide variety of produce; depending on the day's harvest, guests in Biltmore's restaurants may savor tender microgreens, a variety of lettuces, vine-ripened tomatoes, or raspberries to accompany estate-raised beef and lamb and a glass of handcrafted Biltmore wine. One acre is used as a demonstration and education garden, where guests may observe a variety of techniques to apply in their home gardens.

Along with the annual production of more than 100 varieties of vegetables, fruits, herbs, and garden flowers, the Kitchen Garden features demonstrations on composting and trellising, attracting beneficial insects, and integrated pest management.

FARMYARD

Below River Bend Barn and adjacent to the Kitchen Garden is the Farmyard, inspired by the herds and flocks kept on the Estate during Mr. Vanderbilt's time. Guests are encouraged to discover more about Biltmore's current farming operations, and meet gentle draft horses, unique Angora goats, sheep, and heirloom breeds of chickens. Seasonal demonstrations include sheep shearing, grooming and harnessing draft horses, collecting and washing fresh eggs, and the tending and care of other farm animals, creating a memorable visit for all ages.

ABOVE: Estate guests get a chance to meet farm animals up close at the Farmyard.

LEFT: Originally intended to provide fresh produce for the Vanderbilts, their guests, and estate workers, the Market Garden proved to be so successful that it went into commercial production not long after its creation. The Market Garden, precursor to today's Kitchen Garden, included a gardener's cottage (now renovated into exclusive lodging for estate guests), greenhouses, stables, and fertile fields on the banks of the Swannanoa River.

The man, George Washington Vanderbilt, and the place, Biltmore, have fascinated young and old alike for more than 100 years. At the heart of that fascination is wonder: wonder that this man and this place existed not in feudal Europe but in the rugged North Carolina mountains. Biltmore still fascinates today, and is as vibrant, unique, and inspiring now as it was in 1895.

RIGHT: Cornelia Vanderbilt Cecil and her husband, the Honorable John Amherst Francis Cecil, officially opened Biltmore House to the public in 1930. Early tours included only eight rooms on the main floor and five on the second floor.

MISSION

In a ceremony attended by members of the press, local officials, and curious citizens, Cornelia Vanderbilt Cecil and her husband the Honorable John Francis Amherst Cecil officially opened the doors of Biltmore House to the public for the first time on March 15, 1930. Their mission in doing so was two-fold: to generate tourism dollars to improve the local economy hard-hit by the Great Depression, and to bring in much-needed dollars for the preservation of Biltmore House and the Estate. At the ceremony, Mrs. Cecil spoke the following words:

Mr. Cecil and I hope that through the opening of Biltmore House to the public, Asheville and Western North Carolina will derive all the benefit they deserve and the people who go through the house will get as much pleasure and enjoyment out of it as Mr. Cecil and I do in making it possible. I also want to say that in doing this, it is a fitting memorial to my father. After all, it was his life's work and creation.

George Vanderbilt, Cornelia's father, certainly never intended when he founded Biltmore that one day more than one million people would experience his creation each year. He did, however, establish the overriding principles that still inspire and guide his descendants in the management of Biltmore today: self-sufficiency, gracious hospitality, stewardship of the land, community, family, and private preservation.

SELF-SUFFICIENCY

Even with the support of one million guests who visit each year, the expense of maintaining Biltmore House, Gardens, Winery, and River Bend Farm is monumental. To that end, The Biltmore Company has evolved into a multi-faceted organization committed to excellence in all of its endeavors.

Beginning with the opening of the Winery in 1985, Biltmore's owners and management team have sought new and creative

ways to ensure Biltmore's preservation as a privately owned, profitable working estate. Today, the Biltmore Estate Wine Company produces a broad portfolio of fine wines earning awards and accolades around the country. In 2007, the Wine Company shipped more than 1.8 million bottles, supported distribution in 12 states and the District of Columbia, and supplied Biltmore wines to more than 200,000 retail locations.

Biltmore™ For Your Home is a more recent initiative undertaken to expand the Estate's business beyond its borders. Using Biltmore for design inspiration, Biltmore™ For Your Home has partnered with leading manufacturers of home furnishings, home building materials, decorative accessories, and outdoor living and landscape supplies to develop products meeting the Biltmore standards of quality and craftsmanship. A variety of licensed products are sold in the Estate's retail shops, as well as through retailers nationwide.

LEFT: Biltmore Estate Wines grace the tables of homes and restaurants around the country, with distribution growing each year.

ABOVE: From hardwood floors and paint to furniture, bedding, and accessories, Biltmore™ For Your Home licensed products allow people to enjoy the inspiration of Biltmore in their own homes.

ABOVE: Guests enjoy many outdoor activities on the Estate's 8,000 acres.

RIGHT: The Inn on Biltmore Estate® offers relaxed luxury inspired by the Vanderbilt legacy of hospitality.

OPPOSITE: For more than a million guests annually, Biltmore today remains an escape from everyday life.

GRACIOUS HOSPITALITY

For the Vanderbilts, welcoming family and friends to Biltmore was carried out with graciousness and every attention to detail. Today, that tradition continues with Biltmore's commitment to service and hospitality to every guest. For those who wish to experience what it must have been like to actually stay on the Estate—in much the same way guests of the Vanderbilts experienced the property—there is the Inn on Biltmore Estate,® which opened in 2001. The 213-room inn has received numerous honors for its service and ambiance, including Four Stars from *Mobil Travel Guide*.

Just as it did 100 years ago, Biltmore also provides recreational activities and amenities for its guests within its 8,000 acres, whether they are staying at the inn or visiting for the day. Outdoor experiences range from sedate to active, including horseback rides, biking, carriage rides, float trips on the French Broad River, fly-fishing, sporting clays, Segway tours, and the Land Rover Experience Driving School.

STEWARDSHIP AND COMMUNITY

Many years ago, George and Edith Vanderbilt committed themselves to the betterment of the Western North Carolina area by supporting educational initiatives, promoting a spirit of community, and ensuring the protection of thousands of acres of agricultural and forested mountain land. Today, Biltmore remains dedicated to these same principles.

With more than 1,700 employees, The Biltmore Company works to make sure the region is a great place to live and work through its commitment to the issues of affordable housing and a clean, healthy environment. Biltmore's work for environmental conservation has positioned the company as a leader in the state in active protection of our natural resources.

FAMILY & PRESERVATION

George Vanderbilt would be proud to see that Biltmore, his "life's work and creation," survives intact, continuing to inspire extraordinary living after more than a century. With the third generation of his descendants leading The Biltmore Company, the focus of our efforts and of all our business endeavors is to support our mission: the preservation of Biltmore as a privately owned, profitable, working estate.

Biltmore remains a family-owned enterprise, and its guiding principles of integrity, teamwork, leadership, authenticity, hospitality, community, and quality are central to the operation and well-being of the company.